MUSIC IN THE HEAD

MUSIC IN THE HEAD
Living At the Brain-Mind Border

Your Brain Makes Sound
Your Mind Makes Music
(And dreams, poems, and everything else)

Leo Rangell, M.D.

Routledge
Taylor & Francis Group
LONDON AND NEW YORK

First published 2009 by Karnac Books Ltd.

2 Park Square, Milton Park, Abingdon, Oxfordshire OX14 4RN
52 Vanderbilt Avenue, New York, NY 10017

Routledge is an imprint of the Taylor & Francis Group, an informa business

First issued in paperback 2019

British Library Cataloguing in Publication Data

A C.I.P. for this book is available from the British Library

ISBN-13: 978-1-85575-724-0 (hbk)
ISBN-13: 978-0-367-32275-5 (pbk)

Typeset by Vikatan Publishing Solutions (P) Ltd., Chennai, India

CONTENTS

vi   CONTENTS

Did You Ever Hum, Tap, Whistle, or Sing,
Whether You Like It Or Not?
Learn What And Why.
Then Do What You Wish.

FOREWORD

Oliver Sacks

The term hallucination carries an ominous charge for many people: they immediately think of psychotic hallucinations, the hallucinations of schizophrenics—voices which the afflicted take to be real, voices which may accuse them, humiliate them, or sometimes even command them to commit violence, usually against themselves. But there are other sorts of hallucination which are completely different in character and much more benign. Among the commonest of these are the hallucinations associated with impaired vision or hearing. It is estimated that more than ten percent of those whose sight is greatly impaired develop visual hallucinations (there is indeed a special term—Charles Bonnet syndrome—for such hallucinations, after an eighteenth-century Swiss naturalist who provided vivid descriptions of them). Similarly, a substantial percentage of people with auditory impairment develop auditory hallucinations. These, interestingly, are almost always of music, and not of voices or noises.

Such musical hallucinations are very startling, and seem absolutely real: one may suddenly hear a brass band or a massive choir or a solo violin. Many of my patients have described how these hallucinations are absolutely unlike normal musical imagery. They will be convinced that the music they are "hearing" comes from an external source, and often go to the window to see where it is coming from, or check to see whether a radio or television is on. Only when they cannot find any external source for the music will they conclude, reluctantly, that some part of their brain has produced the music. The hallucinations may be very loud, or relatively soft. They may be intrusive, going on almost continuously throughout one's waking hours. Usually they cannot be stopped, though they tend to fade into the background if one is able to concentrate on other things.

This is the sort of musical assault which descended on Leo Rangell in 1995, as he lay in the recovery room of a hospital following a cardiac bypass operation. Prior to this, he had been hard of hearing, but, in his case, it seems that the extra stimulus of diminished blood supply to his brain during the operation pushed his auditory system past some threshold, stimulating it to generate its own musical sounds. Initially, Rangell's hallucinations took on the rhythmic, droning sound of a rabbi davening, a rabbi whom Rangell took to be real. Later, his hallucinations turned to an involuntary replaying of musical memories, mostly of songs he had heard in his youth.

Such musical hallucinations, once they get going, tend to be very persistent, and Dr. Rangell has had them now every day for the past thirteen years. One does not have to be "musical" to have musical hallucinations, but Dr. Rangell is very musical himself, and attracted not only to classical music but to popular songs, of which he has heard hundreds or thousands in the course of a long life. It is perhaps for this reason that the handful of hallucinations he started with in 1996 have now become hundreds—an entire lifetime of music is now available to him in the form of hallucinations.

It is clear that this type of hallucination stems from abnormal activity in the visual or auditory parts of the brain, an activation directly related to the loss of sensory input, which normally acts to inhibit purely sensory hallucinations. And functional brain imaging has confirmed that all of the networks of the brain normally activated by the perception of music are equally (and sometimes even more strongly) activated when someone experiences musical hallucinations. Similar observations have been made of heightened activity in the visual cortex during Charles Bonnet hallucinations.

In this sense, musical hallucinations are physiological—"release phenomena"—originating in the now incontinent activity of the brain's musical networks, networks which have moved into an automatic, hyperactive state, regurgitating music—usually music which one was exposed to in early life, but also sometimes music more recently heard. Such hallucinated music is apt to be fragmentary, repetitive, without pattern or sense, and it is likely to be seen as purely pathological, a meaningless disorder which has descended upon one. Or so it might appear, especially when such hallucinations first come on.

Many patients continue to think of their musical hallucinations in these terms, but others may have different experiences and reactions. They may accommodate to their hallucinations in various ways, and may even come to enjoy them. And they may start to find or make connections with their inner life that were not apparent or perhaps not present to begin with. And while some people may ignore their hallucinations as much as possible, others may study them, partly out of intellectual curiosity, partly as a way of coming to terms with them.

It is fortunate that one such self-observer is also one of our most distinguished psychoanalysts, Leo Rangell. In his nearly 500 papers and eight books, Rangell has made major contributions to psychoanalytic theory for more than half a century. He has twice been elected president of the American Psychoanalytic Association, and is the only person besides Ernest Jones, Heinz Hartmann, and Anna Freud to be named Honorary President of the International Psychoanalytical Association. As an analyst, Rangell is committed to a total psychic determinism, and must at least explore the possibility that there is always a reason, a connection to be found, for everything that comes into the mind, however trivial, odd, contextless, irrelevant or alien it may seem to be. And musical hallucinations can have all of these qualities for (unlike dreams, or free associations) they are the product of an "organic" disorder, the musical networks of the brain on the boil, so to speak, emitting random bubbles of music.

Psychiatrists and psychoanalysts rarely concern themselves with phenomena which (whatever they may mean or come to mean for the patient) have so clear an organic basis. But Dr. Rangell was also trained as a neurologist, has never lost his interest in the organic, the neurological—in particular, in phenomena at what he likes to call "the brain-mind border."

(There is a clear analogy between disinhibited sensory emissions like musical hallucinations and disinhibited motor emissions like the convulsive tics of Tourette's syndrome. It is not surprising that, many years ago, with his colleague Margaret Mahler, Rangell undertook a lengthy investigation of patients with Tourette's, and was able to show that a good deal of what was often seen as purely physiological activity might have, or come to have, extensive connections with psychic life, the self, the ego of the individual—that Tourette's syndrome, in this sense, has a "personal" as well as a biological character.)

Rangell, then, is ideally suited to be an observer of his own musical hallucinations and the many ways in which they interact with his mental life and history. His own musical hallucinations have become the subject of a grand ongoing investigation, an unsparing observation and analysis, an investigation which could only be undertaken by a deeply musical and thoughtful man trained in both neurology and psychoanalysis.

The founding studies of psychoanalysis are, of course, Freud's pioneer works on the interpretation of dreams, of jokes, of seemingly meaningless slips of the tongue, and of the free associations which a patient may make during analytic sessions. Freud, too, was trained in neurology; he practiced it for several years and wrote many brilliant neurological articles and books before turning to psychoanalysis. He never departed from the notion that there must ultimately be a biological bedrock for all psychological processes and conditions, and in his "Project for a Scientific Psychology" he made a brilliant effort to formulate a neural basis for the mind. But such an attempt, in the 1890s, was doomed to failure (Freud put away his Project, and it was published only after his death.)

Now we are starting to see a rapprochement between psychoanalysis and neuroscience, a rapprochement such as Freud could only dream of. And paydirt will be found at the brain-mind border. One can now perhaps hope to have an analysis of release hallucinations, an analysis equally rooted in neurology and psychiatry, in biology and biography. It is such a synthesis which Dr. Rangell, as both subject and observer, attempts here. An enterprise so ambitious might seem grandiose, but Dr. Rangell approaches his material with modesty and restraint, acutely aware of the dangers of over-inference and premature theorizing. And he does so in a style that is easy, unguarded, free of jargon, almost conversational. As Rangell puts it,

> I consider myself a kind of living laboratory, an experiment in nature through an auditory prism … . I have been living at the edge. But a very special edge, the border between the brain and the mind. From here the vistas are wide, in several directions. The fields over which these experiences roam cover neurologic, otologic, and psychoanalytic realms, converging into a unique symptomatic combination of them all, lived and experienced not on a controlled couch but on the stage of on ongoing life.

INTRODUCTION

This story is about an event and experience that kept gaining momentum. First it was a nuisance, and then a curio, then something funny, then became frightening. It then led to serious attention, after which it came to be seen as ordinary. Then it challenged understanding and led to some theoretical thinking to put it in its place. It ended up being interesting and, from the standpoint of how many people might relate to it, more important than it had seemed.

CHAPTER ONE

Background to an event

Something happened

An uncommon medical event happened to me twelve years ago, which both left me with a medical problem, and presented an unusual opportunity. It is hard to pin down, although I use the term "medical" to cover the possibilities. Was it auditory, psychological, physiological, neurological, mental, a sensory aberration, or a noise or sound or tune impinging from the outside somewhere? I could say it left me with an illness, but after more than a decade of experience with it, I hesitate to call it that. I have learned to live with and know it, and I regard my life since that occurrence as living in a ringside seat at a physiological process ordinarily covered and obscured in normal life.

I am speaking of what I can call musical hallucinosis, involuntary music in the head. I hear music, at first I would say all the time. Now I qualify that. At the beginning, I described it as always there; now I say "whenever I listen". Is it right to say it is there all the time? It is there whenever I wish to check on it. Or whenever I am not attending to, or focused upon, or thinking about, anything else. Does that make it always?

1

It took some time, experience, attention and discrimination to come to opinions or an understanding and a reasonable orientation. The new and complex phenomenon gradually came more under control, as it became more identifiable, localizable, predictable and understood, as well as adjusted to, more subject to influence, and finally fairly-well tolerated.

After first acknowledging it, then a period of my reacting to it, examining it, and working to develop an attitude towards it, the alien phenomenon I will describe settled into being a part of me that I increasingly had to admit was integrated into my very being. Accepting that it could come into consciousness and leave when it wished with a seeming life of its own, I also made a sort of peace with it, on terms I will try to convey and explain. Along the way, this experience wished upon me or provided me with a medical or psychological or mind-body problem that in time I came to see as presenting an unusual opportunity to study it and gain.

This book is about that bodily or mental condition or experience that has become part of me, and that I believe will reverberate to many people. It also, I believe, turns out to have a scientific relevance and value that will similarly interest many, not only those in the specialized field of neuroscience but very individual who has a brain and a mind and wonders about them.

I did say that the involuntary music comes on "whenever I wish to check". Ordinarily, there is some interval between wishing to do something and doing it. But there is no intervening time here. The music is there the moment I have the thought of listening for it, before I can start an active process of listening. I am not even always sure that I wished to check. Often it just impinges out of the blue. Whenever I am just thinking nothing. It just seems as if it is there waiting. Waiting for me to pay it attention. Where is it? Somewhere in the distance, usually over my right shoulder. About half a mile away.

Who am I to tell it? My listening post

Before going much further, a bit about me as a point of orientation. Who am I to be telling you all this? Why should you listen? And what relevance does this have to you, the serendipitous reader, who just picks this up?

I am a psychoanalyst. I was first a neurologist, then a psychiatrist, then an analyst. That was sort of a sequence of progression in training for my profession years back. I am recounting my story, however, because it happened. And can happen to anyone. The curiosity to understand it would be there in anyone at the receiving end. Yet my more-than-half a century of studying and treating the brain and the mind, and my routine, daily effort to decipher and understand unusual experiences or behaviour in relation to these, seem to place me in a rather prepared position to peer into it, and try to make sense of all that has happened. It seems like an unusual combination and scientific possibility. But while this makes for a fortuitous observer at an unusual listening post, I also feel that it comes to have significance in a wider area of intellectual preoccupation. I have come to see this experience as throwing light on the creative process, which belongs to everyman, those who have it, or much of it, and those who aspire to have some and to use it. And it merges and shades into philosophy, an interest in the mind, body, brain and society, the links and inter-relations between inner and outer that pique every thinking man, or rather every human. My profession was born and developed in extraordinary times.

My credentials in music are not the same, in fact add up to nil. I never played a musical instrument, other than blowing on the harmonica as a boy, am not a musicologist, and am not an educated music listener. Some members of my family are musicians who make me proud, from classical music to jazz, on many instruments. A few nephews are known in serious fields, a classical pianist, a prominent saxophonist, a jazz leader, a niece vocalist, my son self-taught but a versatile, professional performer in multiple formats, in Cajun, Southwest, country music, and grandchildren who have made good starts with the violin and one as the leader of a band.

I myself am one who whistles not while he works-my occupation prevents that, even forbids it—but as soon as he finishes. My family always said they knew I was coming, and was in a good mood, when they heard me walking downstairs (my office has been upstairs) to the dinner table at the end of the day, making sounds blowing air which were rhythmic, not quite songs but approximate ones. Songs do get to me, mostly old ones, and I can sway and gyrate to them for long periods, without others knowing it.

A Congress looms

Coming back to my story, to describe more of the background and prelude that preceded "the event" that brought on the experience that I am describing in this book:

The summer of 1995 was an exciting time. I am 92 now (at the beginning of writing this, which is in 2005), and I must admit that my adult life has been exciting much of the time (this does not mean without the entire range of emotions, lows as well as highs). In July of that year, I was scheduled to address the International Psychoanalytic Congress at its opening session in San Francisco, the second such meeting in the United States in the history of the IPA (the International Psychoanalytic Association). The theme of the Congress, and the subject of my talk and a panel discussion of which it was a part, was to be on "Psychic Reality".

Psychoanalysis, in the century of Freud, had established that ideas, feelings, fantasies, thoughts, i.e., the potpourri of mental products, are as ubiquitous, and as much determinants of human health and happiness, or illness and malfunctioning, as the somatic or physical world of the body. A dream, or fantasy, or an affect, anxiety or worry, or a feeling of guilt, or shame or depression, is a reality, an entity, although a psychic one, as much as a thing or action or event in the external "real world".

Psychic reality and external reality share their effects on the subject who navigates between them. Humans are guided, and can be equally affected, by both. The two realms of data and experience can be of equal importance. In my early professional years, it was still new to point out, whether informing patients or teaching medical students, that an emotion, such as sudden fright, or a chronic depression can cause a heart attack, which can cause death. People can be "frightened to death". It cannot get more serious. Today, this is common knowledge, too obvious to need to be stressed.

I was steeped in thinking about these ideas, this small segment of our theoretical system, and aiming to formulate them effectively at the Congress. The subject, of what is real, and what "real" is, turns out to be ironic for the saga that followed. To "be", does something have to be able to be touched? The question "what is 'to be'?" hearkens back to a similar question and answer provided by a most successful American President facing impeachment: "It depends on what sex is".

But an issue lurks

There was a complication lurking, however, during the prepara-
tions I was engaged in prior to the meeting that I had decided to put
aside for a time. About a month before the opening of the Congress,
I thought I felt an increase in dyspnea on exertion, a little too much
shortness of breath on walking fast, or straining, or at a sudden
lurching forward faster than usual. I experienced this on several
occasions, as when going up a staircase from a parking lot rather
rapidly to get to a concert at the Music Centre on time. It was not
severe but definite, and I felt it as a possible signal.

To explain why, it was exactly such a subjective experience that
had led to my heart operation some 15 years previously. Nothing
more than a slight increase of normal shortness of breath that I had
felt while playing tennis, which I was not sure of but which had
alerted me, and led to my having my first stress test at age 67, in
1980. The cardiologist stopped the test abruptly from what he saw
on the electrocardiogram, and directed me to an angiogram. A few
days later, I was in open-heart surgery. Five obstructed coronary
vessels were treated by by-passes. There were no complications; the
result was excellent; I was playing tennis again in a little over two
weeks.

The immediate prelude

Back to the summer of 1995. On a visit to San Francisco to visit my
daughter a few weeks before the International meeting to be held in
that city, I had mentioned my concerns to a cardiologist friend who
was her neighbour. He ventured the thought that another angiogram
was in order. I agreed, but feeling that this was not an immediate
threat, I elected to do this after the Congress. This was not without
trepidation, but I decided to take that chance.

The meeting came and went, was as exciting as usual, a combination of exhilaration, tensions and non-stop activity. Taking a breath
the next day (no pun), while still in the Bay area, I went for the test
in the office of my angiographer-friend. When it was over, we sat
down in his office for the results. Before presenting me with the
unexpected findings, he informed me that what he would tell me
would sound alarming but that I should not be alarmed. The result

showed four or five vessels almost completely obstructed, the same as had preceded my first operation 15 years before.

After reeling and absorbing the news for a day or so, and mulling over the possibilities, I chose to return to Los Angeles, to have the surgery there again. This was to be with a different cardiac surgeon than before, this time in UCLA, where I was on the faculty. The previous procedure had been at Cedars-Sinai, with a surgeon who had since retired.

It is an aftermath of that second surgical experience that I wish to report and enlarge upon in this book. By serendipity, the path we will be traversing will be partly connected to those same two interwoven realities of human life, the physical and the psychological, that I just described and, as I came to experience them in a unique way, to other interesting theoretical issues of the functioning of the brain and the mind to which they led. The clinical data, rare in its content, presents an unusual opportunity. Since in this I will be the observer and the observed, my aim will be to be both objective and subjective, to be an objective reporter of subjective experience, and to convey the subjective experience of objective events.

Although it can be a difficult if not agonizing decision to submit to this surgical procedure, the choice was made easier for me by the test results. Almost complete blockage of all of my previous bypassed vessels left me with little to ponder. I had been living asymptomatically mostly on collaterals.

A related experience

It is of interest that less than a decade before my previous operation in 1980, an analytic patient of mine had undergone the first bypass operation I had known or probably heard of. I remember my countertransference at that time, my horror at the thought, my admiration of the patient, and my doubts about his judgment. I remember thinking, as debates raged about the new procedure, that certainly the new vessels would undergo the same pathological processes as the now-afflicted ones, so what was the use. I had no scientific information, just my reasoning.

As universal as trauma is, and as much as all people are affected by it, each person processes similar events in his individual ways. What had been considered shell shock in the First World War, presumably due to petechial haemorrhages in the brain, became battle fatigue, then war neuroses, during World War 2. A colleague psychiatrist and psychoanalyst who was in the German Army during World War 1, Ernst Simmel, wrote at that early time that neuroses occurring at the front, however much related to battle and present danger, reflected each soldier's individual history, his original childhood fears and terrors.

So it was with my patient and his cardiac surgery. As I had the opportunity to listen on the couch to his pre and post-operative associations, there was a remarkable confluence of traumatic dreams or fantasies as he emerged from this early instance of heart surgery, with his preoperative dreams and associations stemming from his life history. His father, a chicken dealer, would take his young son with him to the "shoichet". The patient's memories of his childhood were steeped in pictures of father and the schoichet cutting off the heads of chickens, removing their insides, and of blood running down the table (the scenes and ambience were to me reminiscent of the childhood and the art of Chaim Soutine). In other associations, the patient remembered being caught by his father as he was trying to look up his mother's dress and his fear "of having everything cut off". His picture of his mother was that of a lioness calmly "chomping" everything within sight without concern for the mayhem around her.

Materially successful and accomplished, this man was nevertheless a case of the most classical and overt castration anxiety one could see clinically. This type of psychopathology—based on one of the two basic anxieties that course through life, the other being separation anxiety—is overlooked and considered not to be present in the therapeutic climate of today, a theoretical orientation with which I (1991) take issue. The patient's dreams, fantasies, and free associations during the years of analysis were ruminatively about castration fear, seeking out, coming close to, and then avoiding danger, and of aggressive retaliation.

In his immediate postoperative state following his heart surgery, in what was neither a dream nor fantasy, but more akin to a prolonged series of hypnopompic hallucinations during a long period of waking up, this 50-plus-year-old man went through vivid images of lying on a concrete slab, while someone opened his heart and collected the blood in large pails and buckets at the side of the table. He remembered these nightmarish anxieties during periods of revival of consciousness in three postoperative weeks that he was semi comatose. In the period that followed, he had a recurring 'fantasy-dream'—i.e., a fantasy while he was awake or semi-awake and a dream when he fell asleep—in which there was a fusion between the recent surgical experience and the chicken 'operations' of the past. In this fantasy-dream, the patient is on a slab which he described as a combination of an operating table and the counter on which the chickens were cut. Around the table and looking down at him are the surgical team, his father and the schoichet, his wife who looks grim and sneering like his mother, and his children, his sons and daughters and their spouses, all of them in collusion. The patient is being opened up and disembowelled: a combination of a human, a chicken, and a piece of cattle. The table is tilted, the organs are thrown into a barrel nearby, and the blood drips down into a pail at the low end of the table. Periodically the pail is taken away, the blood emptied, and the pail brought back ready for more. Everything is being chopped off, his head, his limbs, his genitals. It is a continuous nightmare. The terror, which is indescribable, is followed by periods of depression and giving up. Occasionally there are moments of rest.

There were other fantasies, dreams, and associations—of being in a mortuary and smelling the embalming fluid, of riding in a railroad hospital car with bodies sticking out, of being inside an open hearth furnace. While he was said to be near death at the operation, the patient recovered fairly well, and lived 6–7 years, at which time he died of coronary disease.

Less than a decade after my patient's account, I was to be on the same gurney, filtering the same experience through my own mind and life history. During the interval, as this type of surgery grew common, I came to know other patients' accounts, and reports of colleagues and friends, of their hallucinatory experiences around this operative procedure. Each had his own version, linked to his life history. One colleague told how, when coming to post-operatively in the I.C.U., he was consumed with his relationship to his father, and went over countless incidents in which he now regretted his actions. Another kept experiencing visual and cognitive scenes of his being poor, homeless, and wandering about helplessly.

It was now the second time around. I saw my new heart surgeon only once, about a week before the operation, for probably no more than 15–20 minutes, during which time he put a stethoscope to my heart, and asked if I had any questions. I had none at hand. He then performed his necessary routine task of informing me that there were of course risks. There could be infection, a stroke, even death. But these were a small percentage, I looked like a good case, although this was my second bypass, and there was the matter of my age (this time just in front of 82). When I demonstrated my reaction to his input, he asked if I still wanted to go ahead, and said I could cancel if I wished. I felt his approach to be unfeeling, even cruel, but this was easily overruled by my awe and need. I said I would go ahead. I then had to sign that I knew one possible outcome was not to survive.

The Operation

I entered the hospital on a Sunday night for a Monday operation with an ease that surprised me as well as my family. I did not have any horrible memories of the former procedure 15 years before, after the angiogram that showed similar obstruction. I had been anaesthetized quite easily and woke up to cheery reports. All had gone well. By now, I probably had long repressed the anxiety and discomfort. The intervening years had conditioned me favourably to this miracle of science.

In the corridor the next morning, from my bed to the operating room, I was being given an intravenous, which had been started in my room. That was the last I remembered preoperatively. My next memory was a cognitive, kinesthetic, not so much affective one. I had made one request of the surgeon, and repeated this to the anaesthetist who had interviewed me in the hospital room the night before the surgery, the same as I had emphasized to the doctor who was to give me anaesthesia 15 years before. I gagged easily, I informed him; in fact, I had had a number of throat-spasm choking episodes on certain occasions over many years, so would he be sure to remove the intubation tube from my throat before I awoke. The reply on he previous occasion had been "of course", and I thankfully remembered that I had had no breathing obstruction when I awoke in the intensive care unit. This time, the surgeon had said that could be arranged, but when the time came, the anaesthetist obviously heard it for the first time, and said it would depend, he could not promise, they had to first be sure that my breathing was good enough.

My first memory now, before coming to, was a sensation of what I thought was a large metal cross, almost the width of my chest, being pulled out of my chest, ripping everything in its way. I wondered how it would get past my shoulders, yet it did not seem like a big deal. There was no panic or even significant anxiety. I thought I was in the corridor coming from the O.R. at that time, that they were fulfilling my request to get a tube out before I awoke. There was no pain or wrench, and it quickly faded out. When I came to in the I.C.U., I had no experience of them removing the tube, although my throat felt raw. Later, my son told me that the tube did come out in the I.C.U., and that I kept grimacing and clearing my throat for a while afterward, and had a hoarse voice for some time. I had misinterpreted that procedure as taking place in the corridor, the last place I remembered before I woke up. In my analytic writing, I had long felt that claustrophobia was a converging point of all anxieties, and that the claustrum, the space that was closing in, was the symbol for choking, no air to breathe, the ultimate somatic background for anxiety.

In the I.C.U., as I became aware, the care was astonishing, constant, devoted, and intimate. A succession of beautiful nurses, crisply dressed, attended closely, their faces next to mine, clapping my back vigorously, even too much, encouraging, cajoling. All the nurses but one were close, and helping; one in particular came back often to see me. One was stiff, kept away, and I felt caused me at one point to be catheterized unnecessarily, with which I had future trouble. The "good nurse" appeared off her shift to counter this. This was all a mixture of fantasy and reality, plenty of each. My wife felt the same, even later writing a commendation for Wendy, the good one. In the I.C.U., I was partially, I think even a good deal clear, though with many distortions as well. I felt I was extremely well treated, like a V.I.P. Again this was built on some perceptions and a piece of knowledge.

Probably only shortly after I came to, two visitors appeared from behind a curtain, and smilingly greeted me, a man and a well-dressed woman. I looked in amazement. I had by the merest chance just recently looked at the latest issue of a magazine "U.C.L.A. Medicine". I recognized one face before me now from a full-page photo on the cover of that magazine, of the new Dean of the Medical School, whom I had never met. I figured how he was there. One of my patients, who knew him, and who had learned of my operation, phoned him and told him to check up on me and tell him how I was. This was what had actually happened. I said to him now, with a wave of bravado, "I know you. You are the Dean. I just read your interview". He seemed more than pleased. The two, he and his administrative assistant, could not have been more solicitous. To his inquiry "How are you?" I remember—I thought standing up and coming close to him but I am sure from a lying down position—that I gave him a slow and deliberate answer, "The brutality and sadism of this operation has never been acknowledged nor spoken about". To his startle, I added "But it is of course a miracle, of science and of your staff".

I recovered nicely, more or less like the first go-around. A few days of plenty of physical discomfort and periods of confusion, then up and around for a few days, and I was ready to leave the hospital before a week was up.

The clouded state

No one escapes the invasive trauma that comes with open-heart bypass surgery. To me it is a controlled experiment of how the insult of that much bodily assault affects the mind of anyone who lives for a period of time on a heart-lung machine while his heart is worked on disconnected from its home. Or endures an equivalent accident. The nature of the cloudy state one undergoes is always a combination of the extent of the physical insult and the contents of the process through which the individual filters it. In a book I wrote on "My Life in Theory", the last line was, "Life is a combination of what has to be, and what we make of that".

What one makes of such a physical disruption has two sides, the desire for safety, and the avoidance of pain (a variation of the pleasure-pain principle). Trauma, the experience of unabsorbable unpleasure, brings out both streams of motives, to minimize the hurt and to bring satisfaction instead. The particular confusion I was bathed in during the days after waking brought out both. My mental state was a combination of the external onslaught and attempts to overcome it. After a day or so in the I.C.U., I graduated to the next upward phase, to a hospital room with intensive and constant monitoring. Here my cloudy and confused state was more conscious, becoming evident to me in stages.

On one hand, there were a plethora of cognitive hallucinations and distortions of perception, made up mostly of objects or equipment around the room. Where there was furniture, lamps, pictures hanging, I saw sculptures of all types, mostly grotesque and unreal, but all pointing with various linkages to known experiences or events. I saw an Egyptian goddess and other personages (we had been to Egypt in the recent past). I saw a small, round, grinning head of Judge Lance Ito between a plastic sheet and a blanket (I was an avid watcher of the O.J. trial, had been studying it psychoanalytically, had a strong personal feeling about the proceedings, and felt the Judge had been inappropriately immune from criticism). I saw gnomes and pygmies and various unknown creatures, if not scary at least puzzling, but mostly images that I could in some strained way connect to experiences or events. On looking closer, mostly at grimacing, leering, threatening figures, I also became able to see the underlying mundane material from which I was constructing these images. I would then be uncertain as to which set of thinking was concrete, real, the one I lived by.

At the same time, my overall mental state leaned toward omnipotence and megalomania, and was expansive in the service of denial. As I was wheeled into my new room from the ICU, I imagined, or looked for a message pinned to the wall, like a banner with which my children had greeted me when I had returned home over 30 years ago after I had been elected President of the American Psychoanalytic Association. While there was no such item, I began to see writing on the wall. I then saw that the script had no border, and wondered how it could be a note, when I then saw that the writing stretched out and covered the entire wall, from floor to ceiling. Then I saw that it was continuous, stretching and spreading to the adjacent walls and over the entire ceiling. Then I saw that the handwritten message was moving, scrolling over the whole room, counter clockwise. I tried to make out the words, but could not. I attributed this to my limited vision at this distance. But here and there among the words I made out my name, in somewhat bolder print, so I continued to believe—or hope—there was a letter of welcome and greeting and congratulations to me (from the surgeon or our common friend, the Dean). What it all spelled was victory, achievement, mission accomplished, the operation was a complete success—a fantasy, hope, facts I hardly yet knew.

I was confused, and in some conflict over my judgment, but gradually I was disillusioned. There was a large horizontal tag on the door which I read in the same vein, as some personal greeting or announcement, but with increasing doubts. When I pointed to it and asked the nurse what it said, she told me it was the room number. Over the next days, there was moving script on the television screen, first when it was on, then also when it was off. When the script moved off the screen past the borders of the television set on to the walls and over the ceiling, I began to know it was coming from me, not an external message. But I still continued to watch it. After a while, I could detach from it. Over time, it was no longer there. I live and work in Los Angeles, the place of scripts and movies. And I write a lot. That's how my delirious, unchecked mind put all this together.

These were cognitive, with their accompanying affective, distortions. I early knew they would go away. A kind of manic humour helped; I remember when a doctor asked me matter of factly "How do you feel?" I said something like, "Great, never felt better in my life". And an erotic haze, transferred to the nurses in the new situation, along with fantasies that they were returning it. Gradually, as my dancing visual images and their accompanying fanciful activities diminished, I began to attend more to my physical discomforts, which were not minor. This second time around, my legs were butchered, as they had cut and searched deeper into the secondary venous system of both legs for good-enough vessels to use for transplantation. The scars, in the fronts and backs of both legs, and alongside one knee, were mostly held together this time not by sutures but by quite thick metal clamps. They looked to me like one would clip strips of leather together hurriedly or temporarily—and felt as such. With the mental state slightly better, or at least clearer, the physical effects came more to be suffered.

CHAPTER TWO

The sound of music

The happening: Enter music

In the I.C.U. on the first or second day, I began to be aware that I was hearing and listening to singing outside my hospital room. At first it was automatic and I was mostly not aware that I was listening, but gradually I began to attend to it more and more. Where I first thought it was sporadic, I soon became conscious of the fact that whenever I listened actively, it was there. My immediate thought was that there is a Rabbi in a school out there, and he seems pretty busy. The voice was sonorous, deep, slow, a chanting, "dovening" (praying) rhythm, which I began to interpret as a head Rabbi teaching others to become and sing like Rabbis. At first my thoughts were fleeting. When I still heard it at night, and even very late as I was trying to sleep, and remembered that this singing had been continuous even during the day, I thought the Rabbi and his students were certainly conscientious and persistent. They must also work late.

I later found out that this mis-perception had begun earlier, almost immediately upon recovering consciousness, which I must have then forgotten until I became a bit clearer. My son tells me that as soon as the tube was removed from my throat (which I had felt as that metal cross coming out of my chest), with a rasping voice I had said there was music out there. My children had all looked on with amazement and wonder, and tried to put me straight.

I remembered now that there was a religious building, a Hillel Foundation, out there on the college campus, in the general area of the University hospital. That must be it. The sounds are coming from there; they certainly waft up far to reach my window, but so it is. I also heard the singing in early morning, as soon as I awakened. The first songs were funereal, sombre, serious, elegiac, like a continuous dirge, music for a memorial. At one point, I told myself, although humorously, they must be for me, that I must be dead. They were hymnal; they reminded me of a song around my Bar-Mitzvah. I had sung in a choir on that occasion, a rare and never repeated activity. I also sang a solo then, which I uncharacteristically have always remembered. This was a song that came back now. "tvi-ee-ee-ee-ee-anu, el ha-a kaadshechaka, b'motsvoiya, b'motsvoiya ..." Not infrequently, I had hummed or even jokingly sang this solo to my children, along with other songs and tunes of my boyhood days, making up Hebrew words after the few that I remembered. The chanting also brought to mind my father in the synagogue, whom we would accompany on the Holy days. The whole atmosphere brought back my pre-adolescent days, my solemn (yet light-hearted) and attentive father, his devotion and his values.

When I once asked my wife and my visiting children about that school out there, they looked at me funny. My son, an artist and musicologist, whose acute perceptions I have always admired, smiled, and said "There's no singing or music outside". That gave me a start. Another incident that made me pause and wonder was when I called my daughter's attention to the singing "in that Hillel Foundation across the street", and she replied, "Dad, your surgeon's name is Hillel". Hillel Laks, famous for heart transplants in children, had performed the operation. As a psychoanalyst, a signal and query flashed across my brain. But I quickly put it aside.

The music continued through the hospital stay. But the songs changed. I did not realize until much later that they followed, or rather may have indicated, changed moods. The tunes became more active and movement-oriented, such as what I came to recognize as "The Chattanooga Choo-Choo, and "The Atchison, Topeka and the Santa Fe", to me marching songs of going places. I heard them and sang along with them, in good and improving spirits. I did not think about or question them but went along. I hummed and quietly sang and swayed with the music. Along with them, I felt, coincidentally, I was rapidly getting better.

I left the hospital in about a week, about the same time as after the first operation 14 years before. In the day or two before I left, the music was becoming really lively. I thought nothing about the fact that one of the songs shortly before I left was, when the words came to me, "When Johnny comes marching home again, Hurrah! Hurrah!" the next words, which I looked up much later, were "We'll give him a hearty welcome then/Hurrah! Hurrah!/The men will cheer and the boys will shout/The ladies they will all turn out/And we'll all feel gay,/When Johnny comes marching home."

"My God, it's me"

I accepted the song, was happy, and sang along with it. But to me there was still no question but that these songs came from the outside. It was not until the day I left that another thought hit me. As I was being driven home, I mused for a moment that I would miss the music. But when finally, far enough away for me to be sure, we came to the hills of Brentwood, where I lived, and I suddenly realized that the songs had come with me, and were still there, in the hills, way off over my right shoulder, I was struck, and wondered, half afraid, "My God, it's me. They are coming from me. They are in me somewhere. *I* am singing".

The involuntary and automatic music became a symptom, the most enduring after-effect of the entire experience (besides, I hope, the positive results of the by-passed coronary vessels). It has stayed with me from then on, and has become a fixture of my life. I hear a tune all the time, or whenever I listen, mostly without words, which I can supply if I know them. Usually, if I want the words, I have to struggle to get them, even if I have just been with that tune recently. While the music continues to sound as if outside me, I have become familiar with a new dimension of me. The songs come on their own, and I listen. I am listening to me.

A new era begins

A new era begins and starts to take root. The songs continue. They are there always, but in the early days they do not bother me much.

They are generally spirited melodies of different types, patriotic, romantic, or marching songs, many of them sing-alongs. They actually often make me happy. I hum or sing along. For the most part, I do not yet give heir presence much meaning, certainly not a dire one. I really don't know how long they will last, nor how tenacious or distracting they are or will be. And I am able to continue to do my things. I am back in a busy practice, continue to do much writing, and teaching, and am engaged in a plethora of extra-curricular activities.

The resumption of all that was before seems all at once, but the ease in doing so is not that simple. Getting to feel strong and easy is gradual, and takes time. The songs and tunes and music are there, and are of a great variety. To recapture a few, an early song, in the days just home from the hospital, was a sudden experience: at 5 AM, as I am sitting up with heavy feet and these pressing auditory symptoms, worried about both, out of nowhere, "God Bless America, land of the free, stand beside her, and guide her,", etc. breaks out in its entirety: "God Bless America,/ Land that I love/Stand beside her,/ And guide her,/Through the night with the light from above,/From the mountains,/To the prairies,/To the ocean,/White with foam,/ God bless America,/My home sweet home,/God bless America,/ My home sweet home." Though seemingly related to a burst of patriotism, it felt more to be the obvious home, sweet home.

In another mood: a melancholy song-memory comes over me through which I mourned for an epoch, for a whole generation, wishing them better luck than I am having at this moment: "Once I built a railroad,/ made it run/ Made it race against time/ Once I built a railroad,/ now it's done/ Brother can you spare a dime—Once I built a tower to the sun/ Brick and rivet and lime/ Once I built a tower, now it's done/ Brother can you spare a dime?" The tune and words bring an ache for a time in history—I think of soldiers after the War that I was part of, returning, many not to the wonderful profession I am fortunate to be part of-here my luck was better, not worse than others. I think of, and feel for Okies; the "Grapes of Wrath" pervade me.

Another mood comes in its turn, an opposite one, looking up; all is good, optimistic. "He floats through the air with the greatest of ease/The daring young man on the flying trapeze/His movements were graceful/All the girls he could please/And my love he has stolen away." This takes over, and stays for a time, during which

I soar along with it. I am "jaunty, jolly" now, after the great record of Mel Brooks that was a staple in my family. I had obviously identified with the gymnast, not the lost soul whose girl the scoundrel took away (I actually did not remember the last line, who the singer is, until I looked this up!). It is I who floats; I can do anything.

The role of the music in affects and moods is clear. The song, tune or even just rhythm, defines how I *feel*. I can tell how I am feeling from the song in my head, sometimes before I know that I feel happy or sad. I am not sure whether the emotion or mood brings on the song, or whether the reverse holds true, that the music or song *results* in the emotional mood. What I suggest as the mechanism at work is that that the external ambience or the specific event just experienced in the outer world, lights up cerebral cells that carry the memory of a parallel experience and automatically link up with its emotional accompaniment. The same onset can be initiated in the internal world by a fantasy, conscious or unconscious. Or by a consciously-directed thought, or memory, or stream of thinking. The combination then of ideas and feeling, the memory or thinking about the event and the associated affect that accompanies it, looking to prolong the experience and savour or digest it longer, and also for a symbol to connote and represent it, recalls and lights up a song or music that fits this bill, that conjures up just that complex combination of thought and feeling. The sequence makes it last longer.

This makes for the continuous mood, which in turn exerts its pervasive effect. The memory, with its affect, operates unconsciously, on its own motivational energy, without much, if any, conscious control, and stamps the external affective state, from light-hearted to depressed. The mood, thus determined, can go on to have its own derivative effects, on the body and on external action. The further course is dependent on many variables, the least of which is that I (consciously) want the music to end!

I should be able to stop it or start it, to prolong or re-direct it. But can I really? I (we) shall see. How much power, or will, or executing ability do I have? How much can I regulate or control my mind?

Advice

It was interesting what a torrent of advice comes one's way from well-wishers, from professional to humble, especially when the subject is ambiguous, and everybody "knows". My physician, the first to whom one turns, who "knows" everything, initially told me confidently that the music was due to the anaesthesia, that it was common and would soon disappear. When it did not, then, he said, with equal authority and equanimity, it came from the morphine. An E.N.T man, to whom I told the story later, also said it is common and wanted to refer me to a neurosurgeon, "He will simply pass a trephine though the skull into the affected area and remove the focus, by either excision or electro-cautery, and you will be cured".

From a serendipitous x-ray of the chest, my attention was drawn to a wire that was left in the chest after the open-heart surgery, for future use to connect to a pacemaker if needed. "This can act as an antenna", I was told by another cognoscenti, "Have the wire removed". Two independent sources led to my teeth as the focus. A friend's dentist told her that metal fillings in the mouth sometimes magnetically or electrically attract music from the air-waves, and that this is commonly seen. Another person's acupuncturist, whom she told about my condition, asked her whether I have metal fillings in my mouth! Both advised that I have all my fillings removed! This would have undone one area in my body that has served me well all my life.

One also learns of related conditions and experiences. Although uncommon, people have reported similar conditions from strokes, infections, tumours; or side-effects of medication, as antibiotics, or pain killers, or some forms of cortisone. Various medications were advised to alleviate the symptoms along the way: anti-convulsants, as dilantin, or tegretol, on the thesis that the music is a discharge phenomenon; or a sedative at night, as phenobarbitol or ambien, an anti-depressant or anti-anxiety drug, prozac or xanax, or a general psychotropic as neurontin, which has a broad effect. Aspirin causes tinnitus, but could also cause music, so stay away from it. A neurologist I felt was the closest to an expert I know of in this amorphous area, who volunteered that he had had satisfactory results in symptom amelioration in similar cases, recommended neurontin, on the empirical base of outcomes. I have had experiences with most of these medications, largely with patients who have been taking one or the other for related clinical states, and I preferred not to go the route of any of these medications. I thought I would listen to the music, and try to figure things out.

I begin to learn

Time has passed since this began, and much evolution and adaptation has already taken place. A the beginning, after the initial confusion and then denial gave way to an increasing acknowledgement of the origin and ownership of the music "out there", the new reality began to dawn on me, as well as its consequences. Along with "what is this?" I quickly had to wonder, "How will it be?", "What will it do?", "How long does this go on", and more specifically, after a few days, "Does his thing respect the time of day or night?" Soon enough I learned it was 24/7, every minute, every second, all the time (if I listened). Anxiety threatened to go on to panic. "Will I ever get over this? Will I be able to stand it? Will it over-rule everything, overtake all thinking, will it consume me, or my mind, like some invisible, ethereal, mental cancer? Will I have to live with this forever? Will I be able to? What's going to happen?"

The times of panic, I am happy to say, were sporadic and short-lived. I also from the start tried to look at it in more benign and constructive ways. There was, and still is, a kind of humour, perhaps a grim humour, connected with all of this. I find myself making the most of this a good deal of the time. A sense of rage and helplessness might have been there near the beginning, but did not remain as prominent states. Occasionally, although I must say not often for what I would have expected from me, I would have a sort of temper tantrum against it, in private, screaming at it to go away. But more often, to the frustrations I felt at every step toward the continuous distant sound of music, I gradually developed a stance of a search for solutions or attitudes.

To this end, I engaged in a constant study, attempting to understand what was happening with the hope that this would lead to increased control. Most of the time, I "went with it" to see what I could do to influence what seemed like a stimulus coming from the outside. I came to learn a lot about the rules it followed, what I could do and what I couldn't. This was not always with an "aha" feeling, but more by a series of quiet realizations over time.

I found out many things. For a start, I could bring the tunes on in the most effortless way. I have only to begin to "think" about one bar of the melody or one word of a lyric, and the total work rushes in and gets going. It is like the most sensitive remote control; I don't have to press a button, I just think it and it is instantly there; remarkable. It then stays as long as "it" wishes—or as long as I let it. But the latter, not to allow it to continue, is not that easy. It is like a radio with only a turn-on key. I can turn it on in a split second, but there is no "off" button. The power to turn it off is the problem. At first that was quite impossible. The more intense my purpose, the more hopeless it seemed. There was nothing I could do to "think" it away.

During this time, the music went on. Many songs came and went. Some stayed with me more than others. Some became familiar to me, as they held the stage for long periods, sometimes leaving and coming back for days. To re-capture a few of the more frequent early visitors, to show the type, one was: from "Fiddler on the Roof", accompanied by the imagery that went with that production: big Tevye singing, "Is this the little girl I carried? Is this the little boy at play? (Golde) I don't remember growing older. When did they? (Tevye) When did she get to be a beauty? When did he get to be so tall? (Golde) Wasn't it yesterday when they were small? (Men) Sunrise, sunset, sunrise, sunset …." The precipitating events to this frequent mood came in succession, a daughter's big-number birthday-now a granddaughter is getting married, an anniversary, a new great-grandchild is on its way, a birthday, a milestone, a memory, so fast—when did it all happen? Most everyone will know this feeling first-hand.

Another song that comes once in a while-contiguous in being ethnic, and musically celebratory, dancy, like at a Jewish wedding; Hava nageela, hava nageela, hava nageela, vay mismacha- Harry Belafonte's song. It is when I am happy. Are contiguous feelings stored in contiguous cortical cells? Does excitation of one trigger the neighbouring areas? Most likely there are an infinite number of connecting neuronal routes. All of them can be directed by unconscious choices, intentions, based on variable criteria. Is this how repetition compulsion is turned on? Who can know? At any rate, a frequent filler: Hava nageela, over and over, a lilting song and dance, in voice and body. I am a secular Jew—it reminds me of my belonging—I belong, I am me. There are also links to my brother and son- one dancing, the other playing music at a square dance. The latter, my son, also makes art, of dancers and music.

Or sometime, when I am coming to the end of a task in which I have been immersed, be it long or short, but with the common denominator of being impatient and eager to reach the end, rushing along and expectant, and perhaps feeling kind of victorious or about to be, I find myself hearing rapid music to: "Here we go, over the wild blue yonder, climbing high into the sky", as though on an Air Force mission on the way to bomb the hell out of the enemy, like a college song but when I was in the Air Corps during the War.

Or romantic songs, a great variety of these: "I don't know why/I love you as I do/I don't know why/I just do/I don't know why/ You thrill me like you do/I don't know why/You just do". Or equivalents, "How much do I love you/how high is the sky?". Or, "Why Do I love you … why do you love me?" Tunes, with or without words. They come in contexts, real or fantasized, to experiences, memories, day-dreams. I sometimes seem to be awash with all of these. All are biographic. Freud was right about love. Next day, the same tune may continue, when I am in an entirely different frame of mind! Is this another look at the repetition compulsion? Once an impulse breaks through its containing barrier, whether psychically a defense, or organically a cell membrane, or results from a chemical change, it wants to keep on going. You cannot put the horse back in the barn; the genie is out of the box.

For the first six months or year or so, I explored mainly how to get rid of the intruders, the foreign invaders. Music came whenever my mind was empty, or whenever I checked to know if the music was there. When I was thinking about anything else, I was free. Sounds of music or song came when I stopped thinking, or finished talking to someone, or was just musing, or drifting, or going to sleep. Driving in a car with someone was o.k., when alone I would be the target of automatic song. Not always, not when I was thinking. If I was listening to the radio, and interested, my mind was taken, there was none of my own music to interfere. If I was faking it, just to have an alternate sound, it did not work; the inner song on its own would come.

At the beginning, I more than once went all night without sleeping, when I was trying hard and actively to eliminate an insistent tune. Trying harder would not help. Trying to think of something else placed me in a bind from which I could not escape. I soon learned that the key was to just ignore it. It went away only when my mind went to something else without trying! It is like dealing with a "senior moment". You forget a name or word. Trying to "get it" is powerless. "Just let it go", someone tells you, "it will come to you". You finally comply; and some time later, the word "pops back". Let go of trying; drift off; if you do that, and then suddenly look back, you realize the song or music has gone. Gradually, I learned to turn away from it, de-emphasize it, "decathect" it (a word analysts use that is meaningful), works here. Sometimes, I was on a tightrope: if you think about it again, it is there again, and stays again; you have to start all over again Try *not* to think of it. Try to comply with someone who tells you not to think of an elephant! The result: you can think of nothing else.

CHAPTER THREE

An early look around

Falling asleep

The most trying moment, the test of whether I would be able to manage or control this new visitor, came each night at bedtime. Not sleeping was bad, worried me. "What if this went on? I tried a number of gimmicks, as a sound-maker from Sharper Image that produced sounds to sleep by, of rain, wind, thunder, waterfalls, etc. I turned them on, one at a time. They were nice, pleasant, rhythmic, soothing, kept me interested in them. When they turned off, or I went to turn them off, the song was back. I could not "fool it".

The psychic prerequisite for falling asleep is for one to be able to detach from thoughts, give up thinking, and free the mind. This is done quite automatically as a person "gives himself up to sleep". But that was precisely the trigger for the entrance of my opportunistic music, waiting in the wings for exactly such a cue. The challenge became apparent. Could I learn to do one while staving off the other? It was to be an exercise in mind control, with me perched between Scylla and Charybdis. If I try to think of nothing the music goes on. If I try to think of something to distract it, the music goes off but I have to keep thinking of the distracter. When I give that up the music comes on again. There was a night (or two?) when I was awake the whole night, not being able to take my mind off the songs, although I felt they were clinging to me, not me to them. It was in fact hard to know who was me, or is it which was I. The fact is, I was and am both, the conscious and unconscious realms, one the victim occupied, the other the intruder.

Trying consciously to turn the music off became like a game: try not to think of something, and one can think of nothing else. It was funny, but it was serious. At times, in a pessimistic mode, I would have to ward off fear, in the extreme, a fear of hopelessness. The sleep machine emulated sounds of nature, which are supposed to eradicate inner noises; you could also turn up the volume of each. What happened was that I remained awake listening to these sounds instead—if I turned them off, my own sounds returned. I tried listening to Vladimir Horowitz at the White House playing Chopin's Polonaise and Rachmaninoff. Inspiring; but it worked only while it was on. A friend insisted and induced me to see a hypnotist, who had helped him in some way. I conceded, and went through ten sessions. Maybe I was not a good subject, but my inner attitude made that approach at best irrelevant. One blessing was that there was no interference while I was practicing and doing my work. In fact, if any rhythmic sound even began while I was with a patient, I knew I was not listening, and came right back to business.

Waking up

On the other hand, I never awaken without a song or a rhythm announcing the mood of the day. The process of awakening is an everyday moment for the musical entrance. Either a song or tune already indicates the mood, or a preliminary cadence is there, in a neutral mood or on one side of pleasure or unpleasure, ready for "me" to add the song and define how I feel. Or just to do nothing and let it go away. I remember a joke, that there are two types of people who wake up in the morning: one says "Good morning, God"; the other "Good God, morning".

Trying things out

I try things out and do experiments. I have greater motivation for "research" now than ever. Near the beginning, when I first regarded the sounds as alien, I tried hard and actively to get rid of them. I can turn on a tune in an instant. By merely thinking it, the tune starts (if it is one I know, or knew; I cannot invent one; I am not a composer). While I can turn a tune on at will, I cannot stop it once begun. My power to turn the music off is less under my will. I was inventive, and tried everything I could think of. First, of course, was to try not to think of them. Nancy Reagan says "just say no". A direct attack was like Mel Brooks' method of curing a person with an obsession to tear paper. "I just told her, 'Don't tear paper'".

I did find that I could develop some control. If the tempo of a song was too fast, like running away with me at a galloping pace, I found I could slow it down, either by my singing it as slowly as I wish, or by introducing another, slower song. When a song started to accelerate like a fast treadmill, and I was running with it, like the daring young man on the flying trapeze, my daughter suggested a song she sang at a Christmas play, "Silent Night", to slow it up. I found I could slow a song or rhythm down as much as I want, even to a crawl. This gave relief.

I never thought of all these questions compactly, as a connected bundle of thoughts and questions, until I found myself the passive recipient of this series of strange and unexpected events.

I said the sound comes from high up and behind me. It also comes from way down. There are elements of both; it is blown down from above. But it also wafts up from a canyon. In the first dirge period, the deep voice seemed to come from God, or a Moses-like figure, with a long, white beard. I saw an ad about solar energy, and the figure of Zeus or God blowing down from above; this confirmed it for me. A deep hollow voice about a half mile away, in the canyon behind my home, drums on and on. I want it not to. The God-like level changed when the moods toned down. It seems to me that the only way I will be able to live with it is to regard it as a good neighbour, but perhaps not without some merriment, even joy.

In fact, learning to incorporate the music that came my way was not that formidable, at least over time. I remember when I was a neurologist, a patient with a knife through the midline of his skull, sparing both hemispheres, from an accident that had avoided too great injury to his brain. He learned to live with it, and in fact was able to put it to use and make a living with it by demonstrating it as a freak in a circus.

Since this new musical fact of life, I am aware of the mechanism from many angles. One of my hearing aids begins to squeak, with increasing feedback. As I await a new mould after a fitting, people around me, as they hear the squeaking just standing near me, comment "How can you stand that?" I reply, and I learn to mean it, that it does not bother me; I just don't pay it any attention.

Hearing: Too little, and too much

Another fact or insight I put together was that his syndrome came to me in some way related to my being hard of hearing. I gradually came to see the connection between the two. I don't think it would have come otherwise. In my life, I strain to hear. Now, paradoxically, I strain not to; I hear too much. The two, I am convinced, are related. They are tied together. Now I remember: I always also hear too much.

At the center of this unusual syndrome is its hyperacoustic nature. There is too much hearing. I hear where I do not want to. I am forced to listen when I prefer to be quiet. As engineers speak of "noise in the machine", from electrical, hydraulic, or air pressures, the biological machine has its own inner, operational noise. That was why I was moved to check the rhythms I heard against my pulse, to see if there was a connection. There was not; it was not coming from the vascular system; it was not noise from blood flow. It comes from the stimulation of the auditory apparatus of the nervous system.

Strangely, and seemingly ironically, this hyperacusis is related to the opposite existing condition, i.e., that I am hard of hearing. The condition came on in my early fifties. I have long known it to be due to an inherited congenital nerve deafness, which I have become familiar with, and have attended to medically through the 4 to 5 decades since its onset. My father had it, and two of my three siblings, and now one of my four children is experiencing its early stages. The onset of the symptoms of this inherited gene typically comes after age 50.

But the type of deafness I have inherited is associated at first with excessive along with diminished hearing, hypo- and hyperacusis combined. A degenerative process that destroys neurones may irritate contiguous ones as well, or first stimulate, before destroying. Along with a diminution of hearing, there are at first also sounds that are too loud. My son, who is beginning to know now what this is, feels that his wife speaks too softly, while sounds around him are loud and jarring. Gradually, all hearing becomes involved. Later, with hearing aids, amplification necessary to make voice distinct also makes ambient noise loud and in need of control. It has followed this course in all of us who have it. While some voices cannot be heard, and words are indistinct and cannot be made out, and consonants are worse than vowels, and treble is more difficult to understand than bass, other sounds are excessive, to the point of jangling. Dishes and voices and music in a restaurant become unbearable to at least this hard of hearing population. So it is with any extraneous noise or sound, such as traffic or the purr of an engine. An airplane or helicopter overhead roars like thunder, drowning out everything else. Or a motorcycle or the sound of the refrigerator motor.

The unwelcome music is also an excessive impinging sound. I experience it as any other intrusion or imposition upon the equilibrium of the mind or body. One wants to eliminate or if not neutralize it. While akin to ego-alien obsessions and compulsions, the aural condition I have springs from organic sources not under the control of the mind. Actually, the songs are inner attempts to counter this mindless noise, to neutralize, limit or control its power. The mind works on the intruder. Noise becomes sound, which becomes rhythm, which is transposed into music, which is added to by song. I am the locus of all of these stages, and can become aware of any stage. At different times, I am hearing different phases of this sequence.

The volume of the inner music is unaffected by my hearing aids. It has its own volume, and is always the same. My unconscious is not hard of hearing. This is further, pretty hard evidence that these songs have a separate life, that they are different from the conscious part of me, which attends, until now, to external noise and sounds in ways in which I have some control.

It's like a dream

The spontaneous song is also like a dream. Both occur during transitional, somnambulistic, preconscious states, while one is coming into or passing out of a state of conscious attention. The dream, like the song, comes on by itself, disappears when one attends to another realm, in that case the thoughts and feelings of conscious life, and is mostly forgotten. And both, I found, are connected to previous events, and contain a hidden message. There are "day residues", a recent or precipitating stimulus of the day before, to the automatic piece of music as to a dream. But again there is also a difference. There is a different relationship to consciousness. Wake up and the dream is gone, but not the song; the awake song is closer to fantasy, a "day-dream". It can stay on, even take over. But while the song can be traced to a recent thought or event, it does not dip down to the individual life history as much. An Irving Berlin or Gershwin song touches the group heart and mind, not the individual's in his separateness. They reach universal chords, celebrate together emotions that overlap in our human experiences. But in the song too, if I free associate, I can get to issues in the same realm as the dream, forbidden urges, unsolved problems, not unlike conflicts that are repressed and find their way into dream life, sexual and aggressive conflicts, as we find there.

The music always has meaning. Like a dream, a fantasy, a symptom, a character trait, any mental experience that wells up involuntarily from within, the song that is automatic, and the quality and contents of the accompanying music, is an external product with a complex and multiple interior that designates the nature of the psychological state of its host at that moment in time.

If dreams are the royal road to the unconscious, songs are the paths to the same destination for the common people. They are not as custom-made and individualistic, but are designed to be shared by multitudes. But they aim as much for the heart and soul, and personal passions and ongoing anxieties and conflicts, each making of any song what is specific for him as much as he wishes or can. The fact is that everyone has both. On this scale, democracy is built-in. Dreams, however, are still royal for the rich lode they yield. Songs are less full or complex in their output, usually more limited to a single, however powerful, vein of affect.

The two intermediate fantasy productions, dream and involuntary song, might merge into each other. In the late evening, at the end of an ordinary Sunday, putting on my pyjamas, the tune of "Luck, be a lady tonight" plays around in my head. I wonder why, and think about it. Up creeps a fantasy of a Rita Hayworth or Ava Gardner slinking upstairs to join me as I get ready to go to bed. I am Sinatra. Why? Why now? Oh, I had been watching TV, where those just-nominated for the Academy Awards had been announced. The screen had been full of interviews with the usual parade of beauties! The tune did not wait for me to dream.

Both song and dream touch and beckon deep feelings. One day I had a fall that shook me up quite badly (I have had a number of them; these are one of my unpleasant propensities these days). Dressing myself after a shower a few days later, I suddenly find myself singing, energetically, "Mammy, how I love you, how I love you, my dear old Mammy", imagining myself Al Jolson, in blackface—on my knees, as he did, (my knees are badly cut, bruised). I am happy, elated—how my father and mother and their generation worshipped Al Jolson—the Jewish Jazz Singer—and I admired his nerve and verve. He is buried in that giant mausoleum at Hillside Memorial. How lucky I was when I fell, smack on my head and face, that it was not worse. I had made a decision, along with my late wife, against being buried at Hillside, where I own two plots. That was at the time our son Richard died, many years ago (of a brain tumour), the lowest point of our lives. He was cremated instead. I was telling a friend about Richard recently. Suddenly, from crooning wildly and manically, came a flood of sobs.

I can reverberate back and understand this now in patients, not only normal people who dip into such levels on the couch, but also those whose cerebral impairments are the triggers that lead to such decompensations. I think of patients I have seen neurologically with pseudobulbar palsy, lesions at the base of the brain that cause such sudden, involuntary emotional breakdowns. A similar alternating sequence, of periods of control, and sudden uncontrollable weeping, is also common in multiple sclerosis, in young patients without such memories.

And not unlike a patient

There is indeed a linkage between the musical phenomena I am describing and the run-of-the-mill symptomatology that comes from my couch every day. Both sets of experiences are symptoms, i.e., they are complaints that are unwelcome. To my patients and this one to myself, they are "ego-alien", intrusions, foreign bodies we would rather be without. Both are accessible by the same method, of free association, to uncover thoughts and feelings connected to them.

And both are best explained by examining and trying to interpret and understand what takes place at the border, between wanting to know about these feelings (or other symptoms) and wishing to repress them.

All are involuntary. And many have characteristics, or dynamics, in common. But no one is an exact replica of another. There is no overlooking the fact that my symptom of persistent sounds has an obsessive-compulsive quality, a syndrome every analyst sees routinely. The foreign sounds are akin to compulsive ideas, aggressive, insistent, relentless; they resist being managed. But there is something more complicated in this story. This symptom has an organic base, was initiated by a cerebral event. Putting aside the debate about organic, genetic or cerebral origins of neurosis or psychosis, or about all thinking and feeling for that matter, at bottom there is the body in all human activity. Small throwaway lines of Freud's (1923) often come to have large importance. One such was "the conscious ego ... is above all a body ego" (p.13).

But however much one needs and utilizes his brain to bring it about, upon the base of the soma-brain and the rest of the body the behavioural outcome is also the product of the mind of the patient. All symptoms, this one too, are bicameral, consisting of two counterforces, impulse and defense. As in the presenting phenomenology of every patient, the syndrome visible on the surface is always a compromise. More typically this is between a wish, usually a derivative of a forbidden instinctual impulse, and a defense against it. In my story, the impulse, stimulated by an organic occurrence, is contained within an auditory sensory phenomenon, the sound that was brought about by the physical act. The psychological issues always latent and dormant light upon this physical given, just as, in producing a dream, they work themselves around a trigger "day residue". The conflict in this case is whether to admit the unwelcome, intrusive sound to consciousness as is or attempt to manage and control it. The outcome, within this configuration, is the involuntary musical product, tune or song.

While the musical impingement that visits me followed a physical event, a temporary interference with the blood supply to my brain, how it either interferes with or is utilized in further functioning, the elaborations I am describing, are a composite product of what the mind does with the brain. It is in keeping with this that the "therapy" I am giving myself is not unlike the interventions and explanations I employ toward any patient.

The psychological takes over where the organic ends. The ears, brain, and auditory system brought the sounds on, which the mind then took over, shaped and struggles with. It can continue it, let it increase, or bring it under control. It is not essentially different from more purely psychological conflicts, in which the ego has to deal with pressing impulses. As the inwardly-negotiated compromise is never without a wish, so is it here as well. When, after the music stops, I found myself whistling the same tune, this time voluntarily, by choice, it hit me. Complain as I might, I wish it too! This becomes increasingly evident as I catch myself whistling or humming the tunes. The pleasure fulfilment cannot be denied, connected to the ideas and mood the tune brings on. In the symptom, or dream, or character trait, a wish, albeit one that causes discomfort too, is always part of it, a component of the under-structure of the emerging syndrome or dream or fantasy.

I acquire some control

In spite of all I have said about the problems and difficulties, I did learn something of what to do, or attitudes to take, and did therefore over time acquire more control. By sheer repetition, as in all learning, I came to know that "it" would go away, if I could just stop trying, just relax. I would say that by now I can quite effectively cut down the intense attention to the issue itself, remove concern, and thereby mitigate anxiety and certainly any beginning panic. I can get into it in the early stages of the tunes beginning to be heard, "turn my mind" to other things, and get rid of the pest. By *not* thinking about it. I have sort of learned how *not* to think about something. It is mostly a test when I go to sleep. It is only the next morning that I know I have succeeded.

CHAPTER FOUR

A decade later

Part of me

I have lived this new way of life continuously now, 24/7 as they say, for over ten years. After over a decade of living with it, I have gone through many stages. I can say I have learned to live with it, but there was no choice. A more accurate summary statement would be that it has gradually become a part of me, of who I am. It has in fact been a good way of learning how anything can become part of someone, which can apply to any foreign input, physical or mental, a memory, a trauma, an experience, even a chronic symptom, a headache, shyness; any character trait, all can become part of the identity (Erikson, 1956) or self-image.

It was actually not that hard. I have come to live with it as with any other part of me. This is in fact not unique or uncommon. One has but to look at his or her skin as one ages. I do not mean wrinkles, but in my case, one who has looked for the sun during all his younger years, the scars, keratoses, blemishes, dark and light spots that cover and mottle the surface change one's outer look. One had better come to terms with it.

As it has now become, "we" (the total "I", conscious and unconscious) shape and take care of "it", the intruder. What has taken
place is that the automatic activity of producing the music has come
to reside partly in the preconscious. Its roots are still unconscious;
the tunes start without (the conscious) me. But the conscious part of
me catches up, enters the action, and plays a role in what follows.
It enables me to withdraw attention. It is exactly what an analyst
aims for in the treatment of his patients, some (variable) control over
unconscious processes. Is this not precisely Freud's (1923) "rider on
a horse"? Who controls the direction, horse or rider, id or ego? Both;
the two are mutually dependent; ideally, they are synergistic. There
is the human agent, and there are forces outside it that impinge and
demand attention. The two accommodate.

Although starting from the soma, and entering the mind second-
arily, this entire experience is in fact a poster child for the existence
of the unconscious mental system of Freudian theory.

The parade of songs

With or without these complex explanatory games, the songs continue. In the decade since they began, I will not attempt to estimate
the number of tunes or songs that have taken the conscious stage.
During many periods of every day, nothing stops their origin or
course. The cerebral alterations remain unaffected, and continue to
automatically produce their extracorporeal sounds. And the sounds
mostly turn to music.

While hundreds of songs have come and gone, various ones have
reigned from time to time. The number is so large as to make orga-
nizing them difficult. Ditties, rhythms, music and songs have come
in profusion, changed over time, associated with events and seasons
and specific experiences; they signified moods and at times defined
a period or a chronic state of mind. "A fine romance, with no kisses"
has had its day in the sun. As with a dream, pursuing its contents
leads to the stuff free associations are made of, which rightly belong
to the ears of a psychoanalyst. Freud (1900), as the instigator of these
insights, bravely wrote of his own dreams. Perhaps too little was
known at that time for him to be concerned about self-revelation.

To give a flavour of the songs, chosen indiscriminately, an early
one was: "Ah! Sweet mystery of life, at last I've found thee, / Ah!

I know at last the secret of it all, /All the longing, seeking, striving, waiting, yearning, /The burning hopes, the joy and idle tears that fall! /For 'tis love, and love alone, the world is seeking, /And 'tis love, and love alone, that can repay!/'Tis the answer, 'tis the end and all the living, /For it is love alone that rules for aye!". The tune alone brings with it the affect; the words make it more specific and intense. I am not dependent on all the words; mostly, the lead lines are enough. In certain moods that everyone will know: "Good night, sweetheart, till we meet tomorrow, Good night sweetheart, Sleep will banish sorrow." Dreams can reveal much of one's deep, intimate life (Freud, 1900–01). So can songs. There is a limit to how far such personal revelations can go. Freud's (1916) transcendent role of "love and work" in achieving human contentment was a powerful and timeless insight. Another rendition of the same thought, in wider terms as "enjoyment and achievement", makes it more easily applicable to a wider net. People can readily see their dreams encompassed within these aims and values.

Of the song categories, the romantic ones were by far the most. My wife Anita passed away in 1997, less than two years after she was glued to my side at the time of the operation. The largest bulk of the songs centred on her, as "It happened in Monterey, a long time ago, /I met her in Monterey, in ol' Mexico. /Stars an' steel guitars and luscious lips as red as wine, /Broke somebody's heart and I'm afraid that it was mine." The song was not literal; neither are dreams. It was not Monterey, Mexico, but Monterey, California. Nor did we meet there, but that place became meaningful to us, where we spent big times over many years.

Another recurrent tune pointed me in the same direction: "In your Easter bonnet, with all the frills upon it, /You'll be the grandest lady in the Easter parade. /I'll be all in clover and when they look you over, /I'll be the proudest fellow in the Easter parade. /On the avenue, fifth avenue, the photographers will snap us, /and you'll find that you're in the rotogravure. /Oh, I could write a sonnet about your Easter bonnet, /and of the girl I'm taking to the Easter parade." As I write this song now, it plays loudly in my head. It was not an Easter bonnet, but a flat, saucy red velvet hat she wore on our first dates at the Brooklyn Botanical Gardens.

The most startling instance of the power of memory of the unconscious was one morning when I was awakened by a song running through my head over and over again that made me sad. First the insistent tune, then the words turned out to be: "My Bonnie lies over the ocean, /My Bonnie lies over the sea. /My Bonnie lies over the ocean, /oh, bring back my Bonnie to me. /Chorus: Bring back, /Bring back, /Oh, bring back my Bonnie to me, to me. /Bring back, /Bring back, /Please bring back my Bonnie to me . . . /Last night as I lay on my pillow /Last night as I lay on my bed /Last night as I lay on my pillow /I dreamt my poor Bonnie was dead /chorus /The winds have blown over the ocean /The winds have blown over the sea / The winds have blown over the ocean /And brought back my Bonnie to me." I think further. It is the day of our 67th wedding anniversary! Her ashes were indeed in that ocean, scattered at the shore of our home in Carmel, next to Monterey. If I was sad with the tune, remembering the words brought tears. This song stayed for days. My son Richard's ashes were strewn over the same sands.

I never remembered words without the tune, always the reverse. Emotions are less in repression than the associated ideas. Words are acquired later developmentally as well; an infant reacts and sways to sounds long before he can speak words. Verbal language stamps the human evolutionarily, as in ontogenetic development. Birds sing, animals feel, and communicate, but not, as far as we know, with words. We know bird songs, but not lyrics.

Other Anita songs: ". . . a million dollar baby/in a five and ten cent store. It was a lucky April shower/It was a most convenient door/I found a million dollar baby/in a five and ten cent store/ The rain continued for an hour/I hung around for three or four/ around a million dollar baby/in a five and ten cent store/She was selling china/and when she made those eyes/I kept buying china/until the crowd got wise." This was squarely Anita, even after Clint Eastwood put a claim on it. "China eyes", hearing my own version, breaks me up. I know why, and when: New York, rain, not California.

Another strong and old one: "Just Molly and me, /and baby makes three /all happy in my blue heaven/ When whippoorwills call/and evenin' is nigh/just hurry to my blue heaven/You'll see a smilin' face, a fireplace, a cozy room/a little nest that nestles where the roses bloom/Just Molly and me, /and baby makes three /all happy in my blue heaven." After our first-born, in 1941. No question about it.

There were others, of other moods. Not all the music was profound, or serious; they ranged to the trivial. One day I suddenly belted out (from within): "Seventy six trombones led the big parade /With a hundred and ten cornets close at hand . . . " I did not know why, when someone pointed out the 76 gas station across the street, which I had not noticed but my unconscious did. This did not lead to any big deal, although I can find some if I free associate. A day at Chavez ravine to see the Dodgers play was a happy high with my young family decades ago. This was the song that came through loud and clear at every 7th inning break.

Some of the songs I regarded as "pep songs . . . go at it, get going". Or marching songs, or action or morale songs. At times of pulling the covers over me on arising, I would hear: "Oh, how I hate to get up in the morning. /Oh, how I'd love to remain in bed. /For the hardest blow of all, /Is to hear the bugler call; /You've got to get up, / You've got to get up, /You've got to get up this morning. /Someday I'm going to murder the bugler. /Someday they're going to find him dead. /I'll amputate his reveille and stomp upon it heavily, /And spend the rest of my life in bed!" Or while shaving (this is a sure time for the music), a related song going back to my World War 2 days seemed to fuse with the last one: "You're in the Army now, you're not behind a plough, You'll never get rich, you son of a bitch, you're in the Army now". The mood linked them. It is an old Irving Berlin song. He spanned two Wars with it. I recently heard it replayed on TV. The songs fade away as I get into my morning.

The variety of songs was in keeping with the kaleidoscope of life. "Three blind mice, three blind mice, /See how they run, see how they run, /They all ran after the farmer's wife, /Who cut off their tails with a carving knife, /Did you ever see such a thing in your life, /As three blind mice?" I was giving a seminar on castration anxiety, which I have written much about.

There were travel songs, "place" songs, time songs, special events songs. Liza Minnelli or Frank Sinatra singing "New York, New York" can break me up: "If I can make it there, I can make it anywhere," rips me into pieces; it harkens back to my whole life. "Chicago, Chicago" (where I went to medical school) has its own power. 'Ev'rythin's up to date in Kansas City/they've gone about as fur as they c'n go!" I had just been with my son-in-law, Lou, who came from Kansas. A song, as a dream, condenses, refers to more than one thought. Why Kansas City? If you think further, you get more. As I was speaking to Lou, from what we were saying, I had said to him, in jest but not in jest, "So the red states are also against Bush". That's why I was cheerful.

Another example of symbolic association: I am writing on the psychology of politics—and of public opinion—I am focusing not on leadership but the role of followership—people following a charismatic leader like lemmings—the danger to our society. A song or ditty plays on, first the tune, then I realize the words: "Mary had a little lamb, little lamb, little lamb, Mary had a little lamb, its fleece as white as snow – Mary had a little lamb, little lamb, little lamb, everywhere that Mary went, the lamb was sure to go . . . !" I had quoted a cartoon showing Bush as a boy-scout leader, saying to a group of scouts in a canoe behind him: "I didn't mislead you—you misfollowed me." The automatic tune accompanied this preoccupation of the moment.

Songs are seasonal as well as regional. Xmas brought its own collection, from "Jingle bells" to "I'm dreaming of a white Christmas". Judy Garland singing "Somewhere over the rainbow\skies are blue" somehow joined this group easily. Mostly, I had just heard it on television during the holiday season, in a program of old time musical comedies or films. A mood can have a powerful embrace. A melancholy song-memory, mourning for an epoch past, or a whole generation, can in a short time be followed by a breezy, heedful tune that foresees pleasure coming soon.

Sometimes the first line of the simplest of songs referring to special events can take over and keep going. "Happy birthday", or "Here comes the bride", but with individual meanings, knowing to whom and to which specific circumstances I am applying them, can melt me down with their associations. Or the affect can be a pause between stronger feelings, enjoying the peace and reflecting on the moment. "Twinkle, twinkle, little star,/How I wonder what you are./Up above the world so high,\Like a diamond in the sky./ Twinkle, twinkle, little star,/How I wonder what you are".

But always there is a meaning. Sometimes the tune informs me about the mood, or hints at it and tries to bring it out, or teases me about it. There is some elusive and secret idea associated with it, although it may be trivial and merely annoying. One hot summer day, a tune appears, lilting, soothing, like a lullaby, something about "Come, little child, it will be all right". The tune persists, haunts, exasperates, I cannot pin it down. I ask someone I thought would know what it is, she does not know. Somehow I then thought my sister would. She is musical, remembers songs. That evening I decide to telephone her, cross country, in New York. She is in her 70's, 17 years my younger sister.

She hears it, first wonders, then she "gets it", takes it right in, rolls it around her tongue and ear. I can hear words being filled in, kind of a sophisticated and beautiful song, sweet, not a simple one. In less than a minute, all the words fill in for her. She sings it. Here it is: "Come little leaves said the wind one day/Over the meadow with me and play./Put on your dresses of red and gold/'cause the Summer has gone and the days grow cold./Soon as the leaves heard the wind's low call,/down they came fluttering one and all./ Over the meadow they danced and flew,/Singing little songs, little songs they knew".

My sister explained, "That song was one [her aunt] Lea learned during her school days and never forgot. She taught it to me when I was a little girl and we sang it over and over together." I don't know how I would have known it, though it obviously seeped in, and is familiar to me from those years. I do not know the words even now, but the tune has the same beautiful and holding effect on me as I hear the entire song as when it first appeared earlier today in tune only.

What was it about that song? The fall. During the hot afternoon, I was speaking of leaving for Europe for a Congress in Berlin in a few weeks. The talk was about the hot weather—what will I take, light clothes, sweaters too for the cooler evenings, will I take a raincoat, etc. I had the fleeting thought, maybe the fall is coming, it will be cool, and simpler to plan. Shortly later, I was aware of the tune.

I am not alone

As I lived these songs coming from outside of me, I came to know that I am not alone in this seemingly unique experience. Intrusive sounds, rhythms, music, do not set me apart from others. I counter, and attempt to conquer victimhood. Most human experiences are relative, occurring more in some and less in others. The songs I hear are part of a series of spontaneous sounds. People have similar moments, contiguous to my own. They hum, or whistle, or to an inner urge, tap their fingers or feet. If they ask themselves, these are not all voluntary. One feels himself humming a song he knows not from where. Or people "whistle while they work"; but their attention is on the work. There are not many who do not know ringing in the ear. A hiss, high-pitched and insistent, can be more than a nuisance. For myself, I know now that I always have that too. I have but to listen, and it is always there. But I can turn away, and it is gone. It is not alien enough to make it a big deal. Although coming from within, many of these intrusions are not compelling, and not felt as foreign. They are "ego-syntonic", i.e., acceptable to the normally-functioning mind. These varied sounds and rhythms, not voluntary but also not offensive, connect me, with my more pronounced version, to the human race.

This entire story began in connection with a life-threatening surgical procedure, an open-heart operation, and is predicated upon a physical event having taken place. The complicating physical incident itself cannot be postulated as of great magnitude. No grievous error was made, no nerve severed, no slip of the knife. Only some minor and subtle physical process that was unavoidable, that left an unusual personal result not previously present in my life.

Such an unusual onset is not in fact necessary. It turns out that the same outcome can come about following a much more trivial event. This is not unusual in the neuropsychiatric system. Disturbing nightmares can occur from severe trauma, up to such as a 9/11 inferno, or from a personal offence that to a particular person has a major disruptive effect. Or it can come about even spontaneously, from some inner physical or mental imbalance.

The outcome too is something that can be regarded as mild or severe, depending on the psyche of the recipient, as worth paying attention to or as a nagging but unimportant situation that would arouse almost no interest. In fact, in terms of empirical experience, it turns out, as it is looked into, that a large part of the population experiences phenomena closely related to this reported syndrome, and has become either unaware of it or ignores its presence.

Yet to others this affliction can become not only irritating, but also distracting to the point of madness. In a series of comic strips, Lil' Abner was captured by Russian agents who planted a receiver in one of his molars. While first finding the music in his head pleasant, he quite quickly became tortured to the point of leaping off a cliff to his death.

Since I "went public" with this condition, many correspondents have informed me of their plights. It has become apparent to me how many people experience the same sensory intruders, to a variable degree and with multiple reactions and sequelae. Some examples: "All my life I have had to combat the incessant tunes while trying to pay attention to conversations"; " . . . the invasive music would drive me completely batty". "I cannot remember a time when I didn't have music playing in my head 24/7". "My head is like a walking jukebox of music—and I wouldn't have it any other way." "I have the same internal jukebox trait. Many people have some predisposition for it which can even be learned with conscious practice."

To some, it was a springboard to move away from other ntended occupations to go into music in one form or another. One respondent learns to put it to use: " . . . when I get bored from whatever is playing in my head, I simply 'change the channel' . . . and then the new selection will play *ad infinitum* until I choose something else or something on the radio or TV takes over".

Some offered advice: "You should . . . consider learning to play an instrument. Instead of simply memorizing melodies, you may quickly gain an understanding of how melodies are created and become a composer." Another, "it's a cross intelligent people must bear." Or, "The trait can be more of a gift than a curse if you choose to develop it."

People hum, tap and whistle as they daydream by day and dream during the night, for the same reasons and from the same dynamics. Less than conscious wishes press from below, rules and prohibitions exert limits from the conscience. Fusing and shaping the two into every form of creative combination, the mind invents or chooses a compromise that comes to the surface. The tune that keeps on drumming, like the dream that persists, both of which we permit but do not wish, expresses what we wish for and want to forget, what we hope for and worry about and fear. Loves that we long for, nostalgia that it is gone, or cannot be ours, are expressed together. What comes out is a half-product, only partially known.

Sounds

I also come to know something else. What I hear are not only formed songs or recognizable tunes, but also a whole array of sounds or noise. It occurs to me that song is in fact the outcome, not the original intruder, the ultimate after a series of predecessors. I hear a phase of a series, noise, rhythms, beginning sounds of attempted music, then tunes, melodies and, when I succeed in finishing the series with words attached, there is the song. As the mind constructs a finished dream upon awakening (we call this the "secondary revision" of a dream), wrapping these sounds up with the words is the final packaging of a song. Begun in the unconscious, polished and tied up preconsciously, noise is converted to song. The whole process makes the unwanted acceptable, the unbearable bearable; the unpleasant ultimately enjoyable. The Israeli psychiatrist Pinchas Noy (1996) wrote "The ego—develops a superior capacity to organize auditory stimuli, to discern among their various shades, and in particular to transform painful stimuli so that they can provide gratification and pleasure. Listening to music becomes an activity of the ego with a service of mastering auditory stimuli that, in their deeper meaning, are threatening and frightening" (also in 1968, p. 341).

I hear every stage, depending on when I "tune in". Sometimes noise, or a rush of air, a roar, like background traffic, sometimes a rhythm, steady or changing, like waves of every kind and dimension, up and down, side to side, large or small,. Or there are intermediate forms, sometimes barely a song, just a hint of one, unrecognizable, or even a tune deciding between two songs, or mixing up two or even more, or finally, as if the uncertainty has been solved in favour of a dominant one, a regular, ongoing, firm, confident song, sometimes first the tune, then combined with the lyrics; this then takes the stage and stays on.

As for the specific nature of the sounds, some are more evolved than others. Tinnitus is a common example that I think every individual can recognize, if he is in the habit of occasionally listening to himself. I am also not surprised that there are some who wonder if they ever have such an imposed ringing of the ears. Many individuals are not in the habit of occasionally "listening to themselves, i.e., turning and listening inward. For me, I can turn on a ring at will, or in the same way, be close to experiencing humming, or beginning to whistle, sometimes with only a hissing sound (a partial or aborted whistle), or tapping or some rhythmic moving of any part. It is not always music or a formed song.

From sounds to music

When there is no official song, which comes on by "itself", my mind may make one up. At times, with no known music coming, I hear an attempt at a new song, beginning with some gross rhythmic phrases looking for some regular order. I might then add an arbitrary nondescript tune, and graft upon this any experimental nonsense or gibberish words that pop into my head, maybe the last words someone said, or I read or heard or thought, to make an ersatz "song" take off. I might find myself repetitively or rhythmically singing "Yippee, yippee, yippee", or "ooh, la, la", or in a different mood "oy vey, oy vey, oy vey, vey, vey", or a random word or someone's name I just heard (Ju, Ju, dee-dee-dee), in a regular sequence and mode, as firmly and confidently as if I were singing "auld lang syne". The syndrome is related to creativity, mostly an absence of it. I generally have to lean on others for a "real" song, or resort to my own nonsensical ones. This is where I need an Irving Berlin. The dream is a creative product given to everyone, but not so a song. For a dream, one does not need help.

In a less formal sense, and being good to myself, I can be a composer too. Not a Beethoven, or a Mozart, but a diddie-maker that won't have much of a public life. It is for me only. This kind of music takes part in my exuberant, wild moments of singing, elation, jumping around, even when alone. I might then take a word, any word, that either has popped in, or is there from some sequence, and combine it with either the latest tune or some appropriate music that fits it. For example, the word is "Pagliacci", the music Jolson's "Mammy". The combo has limitless possibilities, can keep me busy composing spontaneously, wildly, for a long time—or until the mood changes—or I settle down: "Pa, Pa, Pagliacci, Pagliacci, Pa, Pa Gliacci ", on and on, all variations . . . "Gli, Gli, Pagliacci . . . Paa..aa.. gleeotchee . . . "

A typical sequence of events is like this. A mood comes over me. This can be about something that just happened, or an occurrence I just remembered and brought to mind, or it comes along with a thought I just had, or a fantasy in process. Sometimes with the mood, or perhaps more readily with certain affects more than others, perhaps melancholy or beginning cheerfulness, one becomes aware that there is concurrent sound available, some noise on the outside, or some rhythm or movement from within. With the mood, I hear noise, first nondescript. If nothing else is forthcoming, I may wait until the pervading mood or affect is over. If it persists or is becoming more intense, and time is to be passed, I can turn to the sound, impose it on the mood, and turn it first into rhythm. I may then whistle to this rhythm, or hiss it, or tap it. The next step is to add a tune. I then seem to automatically, unconsciously scan over my repertory, which may be large or limited. If a good fit turns up, appropriate to the mood and rhythm in place, that is it; I take it, adopt it, use it, and continue with it. If none appears that can serve, I am not loathed to invent something that can serve as a tune, usually with nonsense sounds not very compelling to others. I can add words, or more often just syllables, or meaningless verbal concoctions. Songs that can be called that are a latest stage, and are more likely to endure.

Others

I have said in various places that this syndrome, by which I at first felt singled out and stricken, turns out to have placed me among large company. At the beginning, I quickly came to know that other foreign intrusions into the human psychic economy were also responsible for this occurrence in many, such as medications, directly with some, side effects with others, or specific and localized organic episodes, a stroke, an infection, degeneration, or a tumorous growth. Later I extended my familiarity with the nature of the syndrome to see that more ordinary actions, habits, mannerisms, connected this experience with a still much more extensive population, average, everyday men, women and children who tapped a finger or hand or foot or lips and mouth to an inner rhythm, or walked along to keep in harmony with some internal sequence or urge, or hummed a tune, sometimes not audible or aware to anyone but themselves-at times not even to themselves.

Over the years, casual research or explorations have brought to my awareness many other aggregates of individuals within the reach of this phenomenon-that of being the passive recipient of music from somewhere, outside or inside, that comes to serve various purposes, and to be received and utilized or rejected in many idiosyncratic ways. If I wish to think of numbers, I would point to a statement by Oliver Sacks, a colleague whom I regard as a

Renaissance man in the behavioural aspects of human brain functioning (2007), who reflects, "What an odd thing it is to see an entire species—billions of people—playing with listening to meaningless tonal patterns, occupied and preoccupied much of their time by what they call music." (2006, p. 2528).

Song and dance have a long history, and probably have served an evolutionary function since the history of man. People have sung together, danced together, jigged and undulated together ever since man joined with others in groups. Sounds, rhythms, movements, songs, dance have been going on from the beginning, probably ever since people huddled near each other around a fire to keep warm.

Continuing, of precise relevance to my clinical sample, Oliver Sacks goes on, "All of us have experienced the involuntary, helpless replaying of songs or tunes, or snatches of music we have just been exposed to by chance, even, perhaps, without listening consciously. We call such tunes 'catchy'—and they are sometimes referred to as 'earworms', for they may burrow into us, entrench themselves and then perseverate internally hundreds of times a day, only to evaporate, fade away, in a day or two, perhaps to be followed by the next earworm . . . [such] perseverative music has much more the character of a cerebral automatism, suggesting cerebral networks, perhaps both cortical and subcortical, caught in a circuit of mutual excitation". (p. 2530) This from a wide general neurological practise, by a uniquely tuned, specialized observer. No different but a perfect fit with what I have personally observed and felt and thought from my intimate, internal seat at the neural-mental border.

Theodore Reik, a more independent psychoanalyst than many, with a sharp and sensitive "third ear" (1948) directed to his patients' free productions, writes (1953) of patients who report "a haunting melody". Music, to Reik, points to "an infinite variety of primitive and subtle emotions. Inward singing has a special meaning which leads not only to what is on your mind, without your being aware of it, but also what is in your heart", i.e., the cognitive *and* the affective. The secret message it carries is never accidental.

Scientists are not the only explorers who have been stimulated to pursue and understand the phenomena and underpinnings of the musical experience. Philosophers have themselves not let the field go unattended. Oliver Sacks (2006) points out that Schopenhauer and Nietzsche, for example, both passionate music lovers, have contributed their own comments and explanations. Music having none of the attributes or structures of language, no concepts, idea-tion, images or symbols, Schopenhauer considers the outward prod-uct an embodiment of pure will. Here the philosopher knows not of brain, or of mental mechanisms or systems, but, before psychoa-nalysis and neuroscience, is giving voice to an idea of an unrooted, ethereal wish or intention, strong enough to 'produce" the organ-ized succession of sounds experienced as music.

I have also come to "will", and to "free will". And I have offered that will does play a role, a definite and indispensable one. But viewing this same concept from within my scientific ambience, will is only partially free. The brain, both from its genetic givens and how it has been shaped by experience and society, exerts a limiting and defining organic component that the person cannot erase or do without. But then comes the individual's autonomy, gained from experience and further development. He/she, or psychoanalytically his/her executive ego, inserts the final say and determines action and direction. I am speaking of the unconscious, about actions aris-ing from unconscious, not conscious intention and will.

Nietzsche, similarly enamoured of musical experience, said "we lis-ten to music with our muscles". Here, Sacks points out, we at least see the motor accompaniments of the musical participants, the tapping, emoting, moving, and undulating movements that go with it. While present universally, such body movements, as well as emitted sounds, are different in different cultures, and are even specific and character-istic for separate peoples, clans and nations throughout the world.

Daniel Benveniste (2006), a psychoanalytic psychotherapist and historian, came upon this same subject through his individual path and actual physical journey through life and career. After living in San Francisco for 27 years, he was packing up for a definitive move, to live and practice in Venezuela, when he found himself subject to "mournful reveries", coming under the compelling sway of "a haunting melody". As I described my own ultimate mode of putting words to a melody, rhythm or sound, Benveniste composed:

> Hasta Luego Fillmore Street
> You know I love you
> I love the deli and all that is there
> I love the bookstore and all that they share, etc., etc.

"Corny", he calls it, a very good word, in the same genre as Sacks' "catchy". Both words, I would attest, are exactly on target in describing a central feel of this type of song that seems like an indulgence—however compulsive, involuntary, relentless and obsessive these preoccupations become. He later found that the first two lines were grafted on to a melody he had known before, one about coming home, "I'll be home for Christmas". Later he speaks of the commonness of unconscious plagiarism. This is true. It cannot be known how ubiquitous this is, the calling up of unconsciously known previous mental products of one's self or others, which have become the stuff of general unconscious knowledge. In listening to my own my intrusive ditties, I often discover that the first half of a song merges in its second half into a similar related oldie—as from one love song into another.. Years later, at the home of friends, Benveniste heard the melody he had borrowed for the second part of his song: from "La Vie en Rose". He then remembered that his parents had loved to listen to Edith Piaf singing this when he was still a child.

Here nothing had happened physically, somatically to initiate the process—but a fairly violent shake-up of his external situation—a life move enough to stimulate internal, intrapsychic effects. A psycho-somato-psychic series ensued, culminating in the song—the cerebral imaging of the impending move stimulates a feeling of loss and nostalgia, the brain accompaniments of the affect (linking to previous associated responses) bring about a stirring of the auditory system to produce a familiar group of sounds (and rhythms), which are elaborated by the executive and creative ego by superimposing compatible and lilting words, to result in an involuntary (i.e., consciously involuntary) song.

In a series of discoveries not unlike my own, this author went on to recognize that he frequently awakened with a song that was "a preconscious commentary on my emotional situation". (p. 30) The relation to dreams is similarly recognized, the author going even further: "The things that occur to us during the day provide a mental sound-track for our current state of affairs. I assume they stand somewhere between a dream and a fantasy in relation to ego control, which makes me wonder if any analysts or psychotherapists find themselves interpreting, through self-analysis, the songs that occur to them while seeing their patients". (p. 30)

This link to the analytic situation is precisely what I found elaborated in a paper by Hannett in 1964, half a century before.

The author begins that she was marginally aware that early morning whistling by members of her family often expressed the mood of the moment—happy, sad, resigned, or hopeful. Usually only a phrase or two was being whistled but they would give her clue to the mood. She gives two examples, "OH, WHAT A BEAUTIFUL MORNIN'" from Oklahoma! or "He Floats Through the Air with the Greatest of Ease, THE DARING YOUNG MAN ON THE FLYING TRAPEZE". Both songs that are part of my own repetitive repertoire, which should be no surprise, coming from one of my own generation. Often the whistler could not have recalled the words. It was a song without conscious words.

More or less coincident with this observation came the realization that the patient who had been in analysis for some time had established a pattern of reporting snatches of songs, which occurred to him during our session or at other times. These song fragments had an insistent quality that he did not understand. Occasionally he would recognize a link between the remembered and plaguing words and the content of a previous hour. More often the connection remained obscure. As the analyst realized that the lyrics were preconscious expressions, it became clear that the patient was using them to convey emotions and feelings he could not express directly. This revealed particularly the patient's resistance since he had impressed the analyst with his great verbal capacity. It was evident that a direct statement from him would have been too close to emotions, which he was not yet ready to experience. Another's words, the lyrics of the song, provided the necessary distance and yet gave a hint of the underlying turmoil. These lyrics were used to express most specifically the transference, though they often provided a clue to the current conflict in the analysis.

Two interesting activities are then reported in depth. One was the steady attention to and use of this musical material for the furtherance of the analysis, with impressive results. "The haunting lyric" (same word as Reik, and Benveniste) is a 'voice of the preconscious' and must be understood in the same way as a dream fragment, a fantasy, or a repetitive act. Such lyric fragments have both manifest and latent meanings. The manifest meaning restates the defensive surface position. The latent meaning, referring to the impulses and wishes and their genetic origin, is revealed only by analysis of the lyric as if it were a dream. Again the linkage to dream, or fantasy, to what analysts call primary process thinking.

As the analyst listened to and studied these lyric fragments regularly, a rich vein of source material became available. This obviously facilitated the analysis. As the analysis approached its end, the analyst reported, the patient resorted less and less to song lyrics as he began to speak for himself. Now he is bothered only rarely by this obsession with songs and, when a phrase does come to mind, he tries to understand what it means and why.

A second contribution in this same paper was an unexpected scholarly piece of research, in which the author examined the chorus lyrics of American hit songs from 1900 through 1949, a total of 2111 songs. This period was chosen because it covered the half century during which popular music had its heyday, and because her sources and methodology permitted an appraisal of popular appeal, before the end of World War II ushered in various artificial influences that she felt made it difficult or impossible to determine the intrinsic popular appeal of more recent so-called 'hits'. The songs were divided into three classes: romantic love songs, sentimental songs referring to home and/or mother, non-romantic (topical) songs, of war, patriotism, dancing, jazz, nature, nonsense ditties, etc., some of these overlapping quite specifically with the categories I found myself subject to, and songs referring to the Negro and reflecting his place and influence in American music. The author then went on to study these songs further in relation to what she felt were the affects and neuroses of American society of that period.

CHAPTER FIVE

The science

Living at edges

I have been living at the edge, actually several edges, but a special one is the border between the brain and the mind. From here the vistas are wide, in several directions. The fields over which these experiences roam cover neurologic, otologic, and psychoanalytic realms, converging into a unique symptomatic combination of them all, lived and experienced not on a controlled couch but on the stage of an ongoing life. Arising from the psychic depth after a neurological breach, a neuro-psycho-otologic window has been opened to me by this personal experience.

As an old neurologist, then psychiatrist and full-time psychoanalyst, I consider myself a kind of living laboratory, in a position to have made many observations and to draw some conclusions. As an experiment in nature through an auditory prism, I have by now some kind of built-in feeling of the way sounds and moods interact, how rhythms and quiet periods mesh with how individuals feel from moment to moment. I have tried to coordinate the emotional moments I live through with what we know about brain-mind functions, how the complex brain intersects with the dynamics, structure and rules by which the mind operates.

Current times are centering on the neuroscience behind subjective experiences. Psychology and psychoanalysis are being looked at through accompanying activity in the brain and the central nervous system. This is not a return to the early interest of Freud, when he attempted to correlate mental and physical processes in his "Project for a Psychoanalytic Psychology" in 1895. That pioneering study, dazzling in its originality, was on the molecular level of brain functioning, a project that was doomed and abandoned precisely because it was far ahead of its time. Even on a more directly-visible level, however, there is no comparison between the limited data available to Freud a century ago and the capacity to minutely visualize brain functioning today as a result of the spurt in knowledge engendered by a surge in radiological neuro-imaging techniques.

This movement to connect the mental to the physical world brings us back to the subject of the two interwoven realities of human life, material and psychic reality with which I began this essay. To link these two arenas of human functioning, the organic and the psychological, informed now by this new objective data of subjective musical experience, might shed fresh light on a topic of long interest. The clinical data, in which I am now both the observer and the observed, besides being rare in its content, presents an unusual opportunity to reflect on theoretical issues that have not only occupied me personally for six to seven decades, but have been the soil for intellectual preoccupation by diverse but linked disciplines, from psychology to medicine to philosophy.

The present data, as I came to experience them in a unique way, can lead, in my opinion, to a number of interesting theoretical issues of the functioning of the brain and mind. What is mind? Is there free will? Is there will at all? What part does the brain play? What about the rest of the body? Who, what is "the agent"—the brain, part of the brain, the mind, a part of the mind, or can we only say the whole person? What is the role of the external event that precipitates the series or sequence, that starts the process that leads to action? What is the creative process? How does creativity start? What goes into it? Why and how does a poem, or a play, or a symphony get born and come to life? How does such a way of acting, giving birth to a song, or of any universally-responded-to creative product, start?

How does any idea or inspiration get started? Huge questions, but I think that what I have experienced and described presents us with at least some special opportunities to reflect and wonder.

To contemplate an even more general riddle, the very one that intrigued Freud at the start of his quest, what, how does a material thing, an impulse in a nerve, or a chemical in the cerebrospinal fluid, turn into a thought, or feeling, more conceptual and subjective than tangible or otherwise open to the senses? How, when, by what mechanism, does the electrical impulse of a neuron transform itself, or be transformed, into an idea, a thought, a fantasy, or dream? Or how does a chemical process, of serotonin metabolism, result in or change into a feeling, of anxiety, or depression, guilt or shame? How do the cortical cells of the frontal lobe exercise their executive functioning, to result in decision-making by a person, using or following his brain activity? These questions hark back to the riddles that first prompted Sigmund Freud, which he left unfinished as he turned to the other mystery about which we must also marvel, the dynamics of mental life. The questions are many; the answers, I must say, are few and incomplete.

The background science

The 20th century was the century of the science of the mind, a major breakthrough in the history of human understanding. Yet toward the last decades of the century, the initial impact waned, and a huge interest re-focused on the brain. A year or two ago, the larger parent field of American psychiatry officially declared the most recent year to be "The Year of the Brain". But concentration on either brain or mind alone, of one without the other, would be a regression to the past, a return to a partial insight and focus. It will be the domain of modern neuro-psycho-science in this new century and beyond to work out the functioning of the two realms in unison.

To trace the course of the two together in connection with the phenomenon under study, let us first consider how we hear. I will begin with the physical function that was the origin of this syndrome. Hearing starts when a vibrating sound wave stimulates the organ of Corti within the cochlea, which connects to the cochlear division of the 8th cranial nerve, which carries the impulse to the dorsal and ventral cochlear nuclei in the caudal portion of the pons, from there to the lateral lemniscus mostly of the opposite side, then to the medial geniculate bodies, from which radiating fibres sweep to the auditory centre in the cerebral cortex, situated on the anterior transverse gyrus of the temporal lobe, and the superior temporal convolution with which it is contiguous.

From modern neuroscience, we know today that there is an intricate collateral network from this structural path to centres in the mid brain, through which cognitive inputs fuse and integrate with emotional experiences to produce the complex reactions that stamp the human species. The amygdala, hypothalamus, anterior insula, somewhat the hippocampus and other areas in the basal ganglia connect what Paul MacLean has called the neo-mammalian and the lower, reptilian sections of the triune brain, to tie emotional reactions to their cognitive counterparts. Music and song are examples of how these two neural developmental structures are fused. It is in these nuclei of the mid-brain that there is probably a symphony of neuronal activity in the brains of those in rapt attention in Carnegie Hall or at a Woody Allen or New Orleans jazz club.

But the brain, with its intricate circuitry, is the machinery, not the operator, the instrument, not the artist. The brain and its strings, the fine violin, needs the program, the score, for content and directions, and the agent, the maestro applying the creation of the composer, to elicit the total outcome, the musical progression of controlled sounds that constitute a finished piece, that galvanizes the quiet, attentive audience that receives it and is transfixed. The brain, the hardware, is necessary but not sufficient. For the full sweep of outcomes, the variegated tasks and programs of the active mind are the software, the needed supplements to start and direct the sequence of actions.

The brain-mind

Where the brain ends, the mind begins. Social experiences and developmental processes, and the cerebral imprints they produce, are added to the anatomical givens during every frame of living from neonatal times on. The nature and quality of the integration between the two, the given and the added, and their mutual interaction, determine the mental characteristics of every individual human being. But also, from the start, the input of the subject plays a part in determining what impinges upon him/her from the external environment. This then acts in return upon the individual, in an ongoing reciprocity. In similar fashion, the mind does what it does with its brain (and body), which in return play a part in determining characteristics of the mind or mental nature. To repeat what I referred to earlier in a previous connection, my book on a history of psychoanalytic theory ended with the sentence "Life is a combination of what has to be, and what we make of that."

The histories of exploration of the brain and mind have been asymmetrical, while we are now in a period of thinking about the relations between the two. The 19th century saw an explosion of understanding of the human brain. The new discipline of psychoanalysis and the dominant interest it cast on the functioning of the mind was a phenomenon of the 20th century. Psychoanalysis, analysis of the human psyche, sought admission into the science of man's, for-want-of a better word "soul". The brain having already become established as a subject of significant, ongoing study in every country of Western civilization, the 20th century became "the century of Freud". And the last part of the twentieth century has been a period for inquiry about the relations between the two, the executive organ and its social, human environment. At the turn into the next, the present century, history brought about an interest into a hoped-for equal understanding of brain and mind.

As for the mind catching up with the huge advances previously made about the brain, in the interests of an integration of body and soul, a more giant leap was made in this one century in opening the window to a science of human behaviour than had been known or achieved in the previous two millennia. Gregory Zilboorg (1941), a colourful chronicler of the history of "medical psychology" stated that more advance was made in the science of mental life in the last 200 years than had been made in the preceding 3500 years of recorded history.

The 19th century was a spectacular time for the elucidation of brain functioning. To glimpse some of the highlights, Hughlings Jackson, in Great Britain, called the "father of English neurology" described "the march" of symptoms arising from the motor cortex, pioneered the focalization of motor seizures, as well as localizing the so-called "dreamy state" of psychomotor seizures as being of temporal lobe origin. "Jacksonian epilepsy" took his name. Besides formulating principles that explain paroxysmal seizures of all types, he also postulated anatomical and evolutionary levels of sensori-motor mechanisms, from the lowest spinal cord, to the medulla and pons, the middle Rolandic region, and the highest level, the prefrontal lobes. He was the English physician who pioneered the development of neurology as a medical specialty during the reign of Queen Victoria.

Jackson had counterparts elsewhere in Europe. In France, a contemporaneous Paul Broca localized impairments of speech output, describing what became Broca's expressive aphasia, from lesions to the left inferior frontal convolution and sulcus of the motor cortex. Another pioneer of the same time and level was Karl Wernicke, in Poland, then Germany, who, in parallel fashion, pin-pointed sensory aphasia, a limitation of the comprehension, rather than the expression of speech. The result was "Wernicke's aphasia", from damage involving the left posterior, superior temporal gyrus,, which became "Wenicke's area". This work inspired a generation of German neurologists. There was also a link between the work of Wernicke and of the Russian neuropsychiatrist Korsakoff, who defined the syndrome of alcoholism as originating from petechial haemorrhages around the Aqueduct of Sylvius in the midbrain. A Wernicke's encephalopathy can occur combined with Korsakoff psychosis, as a subacute dementia syndrome called the Wernicke-Korsakoff syndrome.

All of these were the background for a galaxy of European brain researchers and clinicians of the era, who together are said to have had an effect in that period comparable to the Beatles in the '60's. This was also the soil that led to the famous group at the Salpetriere in Paris, to which the young Sigmund Freud gravitated for a fateful travelling fellowship during the year 1885. Under the tutelage and spell of Pierre Charcot, surrounded by the likes of Babinski, Tooth, Marie, and Gilles de la Tourette, all household names of a later generation of young neurologists in the United States and elsewhere in the 30's and 40's, of which I was a part, Freud watched hysterics under hypnosis, and began to formulate a novel and revolutionary theory of the mind. It was this ferment that became the jumping-off point for the leap taken by the young Freud into a psychology of the unconscious, first in the minds of hysterics, and gradually in all mankind. History followed.

What we end up knowing is that in this, as in most dichotomies, either pole alone is insufficient. Brain or mind, soma or psyche, either one without the other, is half the story. Music, which in its origins stems from activity in the amygdala, insula, and basal ganglia, the affective brain, also stimulates the frontal lobes, the cognitive brain. Ideas are added to sound to produce pieces, combinations, up to symphonies. Lyrics fit with melodies, cognition to affects, acting together synergistically to produce the total, global effects. Ideation fused with affects together emanate from the human source and perfuse the receptive listener.

The influence is reciprocal. As the brain motivates social action, so does social or interpersonal experience affect and leave imprints upon the brain. The latter, which has been a major topic in the current atmosphere, needs to be received and assessed objectively, not embraced as though it suddenly brings psychoanalysis to life. Mental health therapists from psychoanalysts on are pleased to see radiologic magnetic recordings of the brain produced by psychotherapy, feeling that this brings them into evidence-based science. This, however, is technically and even theoretically un-necessary. Since the leap brought about by psychoanalytic theory and method, evidence can come from various directions.

First, evidence in the social sciences need not emulate physical science, as Hartmann (1959) has pointed out. There is no reason to downplay verbal and observational clinical evidence on its own. Second, this should be an obvious and expected finding. It is now fortified only in that we can finally prove it on a different level. There is no other way for social influence to activate internal responsivity without participation of the brain, the central organ of cognition and affect. Third, there is anyway not the one-to-one recording of experience that one might wish or think to be present. The volume and specificity of experiential input can hardly be expected to be preserved in living tissue in any way that would satisfy external record-keepers.

Clinical, observational, subjective experience carry a sense of qualifying as data in their own right, from a sense of conviction and connectedness that would be regretful to deny. Consider what one would have to make of this recount. I cite a dream, with a complex element of sound transformation as well, for our present interest, contained within it: On June 17, 2007, I wake up in a dream—in the middle of the night—this almost never happens-I sleep fitfully, more so right now with a deep cough, usually without a dream: My son

Richard is approaching me—I look in wonder—he looks glazed, seems to be walking past me, he doesn't look at me straight—I feel 'My God. Richard has grown distant'. I think he actually says that to me too in the dream. I grope for my wife (though the tenth anniversary of her death recently passed)-Richard says he is on his way downstairs to his group—I recognize the wheezing of my cough, that has worried me with my bronchitis—but that same sound now has become he sound of a cry 'Richard, Richard'—I wake up, yes, it was a dream-I am still crying.-with expiratory wheezes. After a brief time, I realize it is Father's Day! And following another momentary lapse, oh, the next anniversary, in October, will be 30 years since Richard died. The unconscious retains a sense of time more than "I" do. The total "I" prefers to forget. And sounds, as well as moods, are at its disposal. The wheezing from the bronchioles, as well as the memories from the cortex, were utilized and transformed, into the affective moments I experienced as the dream.

Such stuff is not for brain records. The tangible and poignant fact is, as the neurophysiologist Ralph Gerard stated, that not every twisted thought leaves a twisted molecule. And Kety pointed out that there can one day be chemistry of memory but not of memories. The same applies to dreaming as compared to dreams (Fisher, 1956). Our understanding of the conditions of sleep and the timing of dreams is continuously expanded, but not equally the analytic knowledge of the contents of the dream. In similar vein, I (2000) have pointed out that the psychological contents of anxiety or depression cannot be gleaned from the chemicals which can exert an influence on the clinical severity of these affects. It takes human narrative, the data conveyed by the human subject, to produce the evidence for these emotional states. So it has been with music and song. As we increasingly see their activity in all parts of the brain, we will likely never see them preserved in any specific location. Notwithstanding the work of the Nobel Laureate Eric Kandel (2001), who, using the sea slug Aplysia Californica, one of nature's lowest animals, as a model for studying learning and memory formation, demonstrated the retention of memory in its primitive central nervous system cells. It still takes a clinical dyad or its equivalent to give witness to any specific cognitive-affective experience of a human life. "I feel this or that because I say so", says a patient or any other informant of his intimate life, "not because my brain shows it".

A dissection of Einstein's brain will never reveal his theoretical contribution, nor Mozart's the transcendental power of his musical scores. However much brain scans will pinpoint where the central structural activity takes place, the mind "out there", surrounded by the culture, is the agent of discovery and the creative thrust. The locus of creativity cannot be seen under a microscope. The system ego, a psychic system of the mind, is the executive director (Rangell, 1971, 1986, 1989) of human decisions and action. It is this integrating system of the mind that organizes incoming data, from within and without, and is responsible for their external results, from creative and positive to the most destructive. While the brain is the locus of physical processes and functions from which psychic processes derive, not every thought, memory, plan, or intention is recorded in a brain cell. This does not happen with a complex, or even a simple creative product, be it a thought, a symptom, a poem or symphony, or a chemical formula.

Phyllis Greenacre (1963), an awesome scholar of psychobiography, demonstrated the power of early childhood traumatic experiences in the lives of genius and the gifted, studying in depth the histories of Charles Darwin, Samuel Butler, Jonathan Swift and Lewis Carroll. Her conclusions were the same: while influences furthering and impeding the creative process can be exposed and examined, the nucleus of creativity remains unseen. We can say the same about opposite forms of special thinking, for the ultimate negative outcome as much as for positive creative genius. Reams have been written searching for the origin or cause for the essence of evil: what made Hitler what he was? The answer, not only in this extreme mutant but for more ordinary hardened criminals, is not easy to come by. The same can be said about the discoverer of DNA.

Returning to music that is our central focus, perhaps it is irradiation rather than specific location that is the determining brain capacity that makes for musical talent. In studying any affective ability or interest or facility, while we usually point to the lower basal ganglia rather than to higher functions, such as pin-pointedly to the amygdala or hippocampus or globus pallidus, irradiation to and integration with the frontal lobes always accompanies the cerebral activity. The activity of the corpus callosum, connecting right and left hemispheres, comes into play as well. The cerebellum and motor cortex also become involved, explaining why music is universally united with rhythm, tapping, movement and dance. Phenomenologically, this combination, music and the ritual dance, has accompanied the development of man from primitive to modern, in all races and at all levels of sophistication and advance. Perhaps it is the ease and fluidity of precisely this ability to interchange and fuse the affective with the conceptual that makes for a Chopin or Mozart or Schubert. Precisely this would be impeded in those with a limited or stinted or more modest capacity in this regard. Perhaps it is due to being more comfortable with compartmentalization than with mixing things up that I am among many who can be subjectively glued to a tune while frustratingly unable to come up with the words that would make the experience total. While this specificity, as any complex trait, is an outcome of genetics and developmental experience, of brain functioning and physiology and its derivative mind, it is not unavailable to being trained.

"Free" will

So I can start the song up, but I cannot turn it off. This may sound like a small thing, but it touches and leads into two of the most central enigmas of human life, the problem of consciousness and the question of free will. Both have never left the agenda of those who study the human condition, from neurologists to philosophers—and the psychiatric profession. What we end up with after we are born, at any moment of future life, is what we have been given, by sperm and ovum, and evolution and development, and what our lives, since the moment of conception, have put into and on top of these. What do we have, at age 20, 30, 40? And with that accumulated apparatus, what can and what can we not "do"? What is "determined", outside of consciousness, and what do we have the capacity, or what are we "free", to "do"? "Free will" has never stopped being a puzzle.

In science, observations are looked to for knowledge. Can anything be derived relevant to these elusive subjects from the unusual opportunities to observe facilitated by the experience I have been describing and with which I live? I am thinking specifically about the ever-elusive subject that has been the interest of multiple fields, connoted by the phrase "free will". In previous writings, I have suggested that the findings and theory of psychoanalysis should lead to a separation of the two words in the usually automatic pair. There is "will" and there is "free", but the two are neither fastened together nor do they overlap. There is some freedom, but total human will is both determined, i.e., bound, and free. The demonstration of the unconscious revealed the presence of psychic determinism, i.e., that much of human action is not under the control of at least the conscious will. But the pointing out later of the place of autonomy, in the writings of Hartmann (1939, 1950), and of Rapaport (1951, 1958), a group of spirited theoreticians in mid-century, filled in the role of free rather than determined action. The complete situation is that "will" is partly determined and partly autonomous, i.e., relatively but not totally free.

What can be made of my consistent experience and observation that I can turn to another song but cannot turn off a current one? I have no ability or method, no radio dial, to turn the sound off at my will. Thinking about that, is this any different from everyday life, with respect to turning off a conscious thought—or for that matter an unwelcome emotion? Do we not routinely just turn to other things, as much as we can, as the best or only way to turn off? Can we ever "just not think of something"? In related fashion, do we ever tell a patient "Don't feel bad. Feel better."? When, after much work, we at some point do say that, the patient asks, "But how?" I heard the mechanism of decathexis (to withdraw attention) described in a debate I had years ago (Rangell, 1975) as being more ubiquitous than repression. I think of this more positively today than I did then. It is big, though it does not reduce nor does it replace the role of repression.

There is a central and constant series of observations in this decade of my experience that I consider data, or empirical evidence, of the kind that a subjective science, as psychoanalysis or any other social science, is criticized for not bring able to produce in its exhibits while claiming to be under the rubric of science. Our papers and books are quite regularly turned down or dismissed from "scholarly" journals or other vehicles for not being "evidence-based". In this personal ongoing study of my own inner processes in the specific area of spontaneously produced musical sounds, I can vouch for several findings as observable facts: 1) that I can turn on a tune that I know consciously with no effort, by merely turning my attention to it at my (conscious) will, 2) that other tunes come to consciousness completely of their own (unconscious) (free enough) will, and then continue on their own, though consciously annoying, 3) that there are tunes, and words that go with them, that I might wish to conjure up that are often completely outside of my (conscious) capacity to access them.

These available facts all have familiar counterparts in the normal daily lives of everyone, but occur in higher doses, and stand out in a stark way in the more intense form in which they have impinged upon my psychic life. This exaggerated form, however, leads to questions and enables some answers that may contribute new insights. The common experience of "I can't think of it", a name, an event, a time, something you tantalizing want, is always best arrived at by just "letting it go:" The answer has been aroused, is bubbling around, or undergoing some electrical impulse along a neuron, or in a region or nucleus of the brain, and will "pop up". More officially "creative" individuals, struggling to compose, invent, come up with a new answer or connection, a scientist seeking a formula, a musician a sequence of notes, a painter a combination of forms and colours, all do best by suspending attention, giving themselves up to reverie, uncertainty, ambiguity. In a dream, or a dreamy state, musing, floating in one's thoughts, are the times of invention, or inspiration. I am adding this very section on will to the otherwise-finished book after having fallen asleep watching television, rousing myself to finish my toiletries and go to bed, when this particular subject came rushing to me that I am now writing down. I first put down the whole jumble of ideas around midnight. I am polishing them up, and making them fit together the next day, in broad daylight.

To look at the full data again, the empirical facts of my observational study from which I will try to draw conclusions, those that have proven to be constant are these. I can turn on a tune that I know, and can then turn this off at my (conscious) will. When I am thinking of nothing, a tune can come to me that "I" do not turn on or want. These "I" cannot turn off, however much I may wish to do so. But I can turn to another song which operates to make the unwelcome tune disappear. Actually, there may be some seconds of competition, during which it is a matter of how strongly I can hang on to my own song, the one that I (consciously) brought to the stage. Trouble is with this contest that I might now actually wish for the rebellious song that started unwanted from down below.

I cannot (easily) write a new song with conscious attention, but new tunes, tones and sequences come up with no struggle when they are emanating from my unconsciousness, i.e., when I am not trying consciously to sing or hear a musical production. And tunes that I want to hear but cannot think of can become available if I start the quest and then just relax and let them come.

The clarity, regularity and intensity of these experiences, while making me feel picked upon by the unusual, have in reality united me with the ordinary, only more so, and therefore in a special way. Their steadiness and predictability allowed me to confront and note these characteristics over a sustained and controlled period, sufficient to enable me to think they are laws of human mentation (of thinking and feeling, cognition and affects, consciousness and its absence, pathognomonic centres of being human).

Putting together these empirical data and observable facts, the sense they make seems to be this running conclusion: Creative thought processes, the images of imagination, new musical sequences or word arrangements, new discoveries, concepts or ideas, poems, explanations, artistic creations, come more from the unconscious stream of ideation and affect than from conscious determination to produce them. The conscious mind polishes them up, makes them coherent, compatible, one cohesive product. It is akin to the ego that puts together the dream upon awakening, uniting and ordering the scattered dream thoughts that have occupied the last few minutes or even a longer time before awakening.

On the other side of the coin, the truly or successfully creative are in fact less bound by conscious furrowed channels from which they are unable to escape. They may have less restricting memories to warn them, fewer rigid paths of what is safe, fewer and less strict superego rules and regulations, or even weaker instinctual impulses to lead them into traditional, universal directions, in other words, less organized or guiding or restrictive inner given structures, from the instinctual impulses of the id, or the accustomed paths of mastery from the ego, or the "thou musts" from a stern and "without playfulness" quality of the superego. These areas of limitation might make for a weird or queer or odd one, but an individual able to find and forge a new direction. Van Gogh is a far-out example, going as far as an insane asylum. He is not the "normal" type I am thinking about.

As I think of this question, "where do original, new, creative, ideas come from?", and the answer I am evolving, everywhere I turn, every era I think about, provides its own interest, data and opinions on the same question. It is timeless, both the subject and the search. Creativity, being a skill beyond survival, would also seem to be closely related to what makes human beings human. It does not, incidentally, overlap with normal. The label of creativity actually is not confined to the adaptive or useful but can apply to psychopathology as well. Symptoms can also reach very creative forms. And dreams and fantasies, on the normal side, can dip easily into psychopathology.

In the sixties, when I (1967) myself was writing on 'the human core", from many directions, there were several papers by two good friends David Beres and Jacob Arlow devoted to the same area of wonder.

Beres (1960), writing on "the psychoanalytic psychology of imagination", goes beyond the Oxford Dictionary definition, "the action of imagining or forming a mental concept of what is not actually present to the senses". To Beres, "imagination is the capacity to form a mental representation of an absent object, affect, body function, or instinctual drive". (p. 253) Imagination is "a ubiquitous process which includes creative imagination and imagery and whose products cover a wide range of psychic manifestations." (p. 254) The symbol, the fantasy, the thought, the dream, products of human imagination, are to the psychoanalyst what the electrocardiograph tracing is to the cardiologist or the microscopic specimen to the pathologist.

Later, writing on the humanness of human beings, Beres (1968) calls upon Freud's monumental structural theory of psychoanalysis, the division of the psyche into the systems id, ego, and superego, and from this base, points to "the concept of a mediating factor, the functions of ego and superego, between drive impulses and their consummation in human psychic activity" (p. 490) as the most illuminating contribution to account for being human. Looking into present and future history, Beres continues, "That man has, even now, the capacity to govern himself, to integrate his drives, his ego functions, and his superego ideals and prohibitions, I do not doubt; [injecting a societal injunction] that he will accomplish this before he destroys himself, I cannot say. In this choice lies the humanness of human beings." (p. 320)

I (1967) have also addressed this enigmatic question, and have come to an overlapping area, the realm of unconscious intrapsychic conflicts, as the succinct domain of pathognomonic human psychic activity. Actually, more than conflicts are involved. This is also the psychological armature from which, at one point, after the signal of either anxiety or safety is received, the ego is at the point of instigating further direction of actions or reactions. Here is the moment of creativity and adaptation in addition to conflict resolution. Elaborating Freud's (1926) unconscious signal process of testing for anxiety, I (1969) have enumerated some 14 steps that make up "the intrapsychic process", which contains this internal sequence of mental activities. It is this wider "intrapsychic process" that I have designated "the human core". Traversing as it does beyond its protective, survival function to the infinite proactive, creative levels achieved over time (Rangell, 1990), this automatic internal scanning process, in its total breadth, distinguishes human mentation from related partial, primitive processes in lower forms on the evolutionary scale.

Arlow (1969), in the same general psychological area, focuses on the role of unconscious fantasy as the individualistic creative product of every person, in both pathological and normal behaviour. Exposing such fantasies in his clinical work, this author stresses the ubiquitous intrusion of unconscious fantasy into conscious experience, from symptom-formation to dreams and the psychopathology of everyday life. At an earlier time, and more specifically, Anna Freud demonstrated the connection between social maladjustment, delinquency, and distorted ego functioning, on the one hand, and the effects of repressed masturbation fantasies on the other. No sharp line of distinction, Arlow states, can be made between conscious and unconscious fantasies. It seems more appropriate to speak of fantasies which are fended off to a greater or lesser extent, bearing in mind that the role of defense may change radically with circumstances. Fantasies are not exclusively vehicles for discharge of the instinctual energies of the id. The ego and superego play a part in their formation. The contribution which unconscious fantasy makes to conscious experience may be dominated by defensive, adaptive, and self-punitive trends as well. Fantasy activity, conscious or unconscious, is a constant feature of mental life. The private world of daydreams is characteristic for each individual, representing his secret rebellion against reality and against the need to renounce instinctual gratification.

Such are the concerns of psychoanalysts, focusing in on the shadowy interests and motivational streams that affect conscious decisions and behaviour from the cloudy backgrounds of mental life. People live more than they wish to know in the world of in-between, between the real and the imaginary, the actual and the symbolic. Many chronic psychic "solutions" result in much of life being lived in the make-believe world. A patient I (1952) once treated who suffered from a doll phobia (a male adult, not a female child), was constantly aware of mannequins, sculpted figures and carvings, besides the dolls. It was often a moment of a figure threatening to or looking like it was coming to life that was the most frightening-like a sculpted bar of soap that began to dissolve. I mentioned early in this essay, in the case of a man undergoing the first heart surgery I knew of, the castration anxiety he experienced coming out of the surgery. This is also something primitively human, a dread quite universal but well repressed. It operates widely, not only in our frequent wars-but also in regular life. My well-functioning adult patient, phobic of doll figures, experienced the major anxiety with the doll when the lifeless figure was seen nude, between the legs. These human forms, constructed to imitate but be false, never have a genital; the perineum is starkly flat; this is the point of maximum anxiety, to terror.

Playing life with constructed figures actually has a deep, universal resonance, positive and negative, invented and feared, representing mastery over the possibility of helpless trauma. As such, it forms a certain genre of entertainment. Since the 18th century, Bunraku national puppetry art in Japan was used to express, through narration and music, the core of human feelings and action. The views to which the audience fastened were not unlike the dolls of my phobic patient, who looked for, watched for, sought out and feared figures of all kinds between life and make-believe. The wood and fabric puppets, three-feet high, used to emulate both ordinary and mythic life in popular entertainment, were finely carved, some with moveable eyes, eyebrows and mouths. Making a comeback now, they are skilfully manipulated, while the operators, the puppeteers themselves, are also seen alongside and behind the ornate and life-like puppets, adding to the ambiguous look on the stage. Virtually unchanged over three or four centuries, the art is hailed as "an intangible cultural asset" in its native country and "a masterpiece of the oral and intangible heritage of humanity" by UNESCO. The great 18th century Bunraku playwright Chikamatsu Monzaemon summed up the appeal: "Art exists in the slender margin between the real and the unreal" (Blumenthal, 1997, p. A3). Salvador Dali is a current iconic example.

The quest for the new and creative, even the startling, transcends art and extends voluminously into the commercial world. A creative advertising director, Matt Reiner (Smith, 2007), gives advice to a novice seeking ideas for her first ad campaign, "Stop thinking about it, and suddenly it will pop up", he admonishes, "Creativity is a process, and you can't force it". How does he get his own ideas? He sometimes "takes a nap", or ideas come in the gym, or when he is walking, and he can become "inundated with ideas. They just sneak up on you". Instead of noting them down, he calls his phone number and leaves a message. At those times, it feels as if ideas are coming from outside him. He doesn't want to talk about it lest it disappears. There is nothing more mysterious. From elsewhere, Albert Einstein is quoted, "The most beautiful experience we can have is the mysterious. It is the fundamental emotion which stands in the cradle of true art and true science".

I have come to this mysterious aspect myself. In my (1978) paper on "the creative thrust ", I wrote: "Sylvano Arieti (1976), in his book on creativity, states that 'after all that is known about the creative process, the magic synthesis of conscious and unconscious, primary and secondary processes which go into it continues to remain a mystery. The creative person remains the keeper of the secret of what makes his personality creative-a secret that he cannot reveal to himself or to others". I have heard artists discussing their work pull back when asked what it 'means' or what is behind it. The artist knows as little about what went into it as does the viewer. It is each one to himself, the doer and the viewer, each dipping into his own psychic core to know and feel what the experience does for him. When the work makes contact with a collective core, with universal conflicts, with the wishes, hopes and anxieties of the times, it achieves a larger dimension of notice and interest." (Rangell, 1978, p. 43.)

If the last century contributed anything enduring, it is that the mind does not overlap with consciousness. The songs that visit me come into consciousness from somewhere else, from the dynamic unconscious. The brain and mind, the body too, are acting together in a circumscribed area of functioning, the auditory aspect of sensory life, producing a particular, unusual form of hearing. Psychosomatic and somatopsychic operate in unison, stimulation being exchanged and fused in both directions. The duality of mind and body, organic and mental, the psychosomatic unity, the fusion of ideas and emotions, of the subjective and objective, the confluent and mutually supplemental functioning operative in the hearing phenomenon I am describing, typify how the human being operates in many aspects of being human. "Use your brain" is matched by "use your imagination", whether about visual images to a painter, or of a succession of variable auditory phrases to a composer. Where too much imagination, accompanied by a loss of reality function, leads to delusions or hallucinations, anti-psychotic or other psychopharmacologic agents are used to suppress the image-making—usually at the expense of a normal amount of this desirable functioning, which includes dreaming, day-dreaming, creating and inventing.

In this instance, the connecting links between conscious and unconscious thinking, which make for a feeling of wholeness, appear to be severed, so that the consciously experiencing ego is under the quasi-delusion that part of him is another person. Surely, this disassociation of part of the self must have representation in brain circuits, that in some way the linkages of stimuli from the unconscious have been disconnected from other input to the ego that indicate the complete person.

My sounds are hallucinatory, i.e., they come from inside me. They are not from the outside, from external physical sound waves. An interesting, evidence-based check on this deduction is the finding I reported that my hearing aids have no effect on this new, mentally-engineered, imaginary sound, constructed to emulate memory. My aids do not affect the volume of these internal reverberations; they have no relevance here. "Realness" is not in question, as per the issue of material and psychic realities with which I started this paper even before the crucial surgery. The externally real sound gets louder or softer, the mentally, not physically real, is impervious to external influence. Inner hearing is not impaired. It is always the same, audible volume. It does not go through the organ of Corti.

What can we extrapolate from this experience to the more common syndrome of "hearing voices"? Again, where these are psychotic delusions, they are outside the check of external reality; they are born and exist within the psychic apparatus. Here as elsewhere, however, it is not all or none, and the imperviousness to reality is not for all time. The human psyche is astonishingly malleable, and can in many ways, from any direction, be brought under the control of the reality principle. That is the hope, aim and rationale for treatment procedures: one can "learn" (from analysis or otherwise) to link rationally with the external world.

When insight is gained, and the voices, as in my case the music, can be understood as to their actual roots and connections, the receptor hearer can loosen or free his automatic false relationship to the immaterial sound, voice or song, and hearken more to the external reality of his surround. One can gain at least partial control over many forms of previously automatic psychic phenomena, often those which seemed quite unassailable to their sufferers before. As I have described with my own musical hallucinosis, such new control can also be seen against auditory hallucinations that are vocal, or even more commonly against pressing, obsessive thoughts, or affects that are relentless and pathological.

There is another accompanying issue, which intrudes especially in the instances of more malignant dissociations between conscious and unconscious, as in psychotic hallucinations completely separated from external reality. To the extent that this split can be overcome with insight gained, one also acquires a commensurate accountability for his external behaviour. But here too, as in many other accepted polarities, I believe there is often a grey area rather than a clear line of differentiation. I do not feel that the diagnosis of psychosis automatically absolves the bearer of abnormal thoughts of all responsibility for his actions.

Musings on the creative process

While focusing on the specific production of unwelcome tunes, music, songs, I came to think that my reflections on the mechanisms involved related to a wider swath of psychosomatic activity. One was the subject of will just described, another the area of human creativity. What makes these songs led me to what is talent, what is a creative act, what makes a Beethoven, what causes a Hitler? In a general sense, this question points to the two contiguous areas of neuroscience and psychoanalysis, the physical and mental explanatory systems of behaviour regulation of man. In spite of the huge advances in each in the last two centuries, both are confronted by much larger questions than they can yet solve.

It has been amply agreed, although it is not articulated with great frequency, that as staggering as the brain is as a computer, which can never be duplicated by an artificial instrument, it nevertheless contains an intrinsic limitation and cannot be looked to for a total explanation of human activity. I have stated, and have quoted Seymour Kety (1960) to this effect, that there can be a neurophysiology of sleep, or of dreaming, but there will never be, on an EEG or MRI or a slide of the brain, the demonstration of a dream. I have never heard this statement refuted, or even disputed. The same applies to a thought; Ralph Gerard (1959) is the author here. Not every twisted thought, he says of psychopathology, results in a twisted molecule. I add: nor any untwisted or clear thought as well; the same applies to every normal mental product as to the distorted or twisted ones. The brain simply does not record every aspect of every frame of an ongoing life.

People "know" there is something else, part of, alongside of and outside of the brain. Putting aside the turn to religion, spirituality or the occult, I elect to stay, in the context of this discussion, with science, with all its problems. Charles Brenner (2002), as persistent a scientific thinker as there is in the science of the mind, characterized psychoanalysis as residing within natural science. Nature, he said, makes no exceptions. While as a discussant to his paper I (2002) agreed with this opinion, I also feel that it is a natural science separate and apart from its physical counterparts. Can anyone dispute that mental phenomena cannot be as subject to measurement, quantification, visibility or demonstrability as elements in the physical sciences? Yet the mental is as natural as the physical. Is mental not part of human *nature*? Is human nature not "natural"?

While we know with awesome focus where aphasia or anomia reside, can any narrative which defines and explains the contents of one's suffering be recorded as such and demonstrated in the human brain—or on any organ? The results of anxieties can be followed, to an ulcer, or hypertension or a myriad of effects on any organ system, but can a narrative account of the subjective content behind the affect be read on brain tissue as are the hieroglyphics on an ancient stone? What we find about our music applies to every form of human mental creativity: the creative paths are infinite, their central registration for others to see inchoate.

The same answer to the same question applies to the body as to the brain. An impressive number of specific discoveries about organic pathology have not been matched by an equal explanation to questions relating to non-material functioning. Visible organic, somatic demonstrations are available to the senses, to satisfactorily explain diabetes, or acromegaly, or gout, Mongolism and now Huntington's chorea. But while a simple and mild drug can result in the amelioration of anxiety, or one of many specific medications can counteract depression, can we ever see the ideational or experiential contents of anxiety, guilt or shame, or any dysphoric affect on a PET scan?

There is ample room for the concept of "mind". Impressions, visual, auditory, kinaesthetic experiences of the external world that surrounds the envelope of skin that separate the person from his environment penetrate the brain, are stored there and put to use there. Resulting products are directed back to the surround. The intermediate activities connecting the two, the images invented by the human imagination, the fantasies, thoughts, mental experiments tried continuously, defy any instrument aiming to inspect them. They are known only by reportage and by inference.

The theory of psychoanalysis has filled in the structure and functioning of that mind, the mental area of being human, in its individualistic, complex, multidimensional forms consonant with the phenomena this total theoretical system was constructed to explain. While the birth of this new science was stimulated by the challenge to understand and control psychopathology, its reach came to embrace the normal as well, the entire span of mental functioning.

I have been looking at and beneath a song. But the same thinking can guide us to the soil and substructure of any parallel psychic product. Can we not say now that cerebral cells, or central nervous system neurons, or electrical currents coursing through a nerve, or body chemicals that facilitate conduction across synapses, however some internal agent arranges or orders them, cannot of themselves produce a poem?

All of these are necessary but not sufficient. It takes a mind. There is, indeed, no mind without a brain. When the brain dies, so does the mind. But a brain without a mind, an infant in whom mentation (mentalization is the word used today) never starts, is an incomplete human.

A poem, or a painting, or a symphony, cannot begin to be conceived without all of the physical machinery, but this alone is not enough. The mind has the rest—and a special mind for special outpourings. Every person has all of these in different amounts, qualities and proportions. But there was one Einstein, or Shakespeare, or Mozart, Beethoven, or Schubert. Their specialness, the talent or ability, does not take a stain that is visible on a slide, or in a radiologic slice or an MRI. The same obtains at the other end of the spectrum, for the brain or mind of a Himmler or Mengele or any other negative aberration. We cannot see the creative act, positive or negative, at its source, only its outcome. But the creative act is not elite. In its essence it is available to the average individual. Everyone can dream, or think his own constructed original scenario, his fantasy.

The brain supplies the sounds and scenes. The person, his mind, within the mind ultimately the system ego, writes and directs the performance. The id and the superego of the mind, and the cognitive as well as the affective centres of the brain, are the supporting cast, the suppliers of the necessary ingredients and actors. The ego (not meaning brashness, but the psychic system ego of psychoanalytic structural theory) is the agent, the executive agent in directing instinctual impulses and forces from all other sources, and the moral agent, in selecting and coordinating the range of superego values. It also chooses and brings about body reactions and purposeful activity and behaviour. Muscles do not initiate their actions, the person's mind, and within that the ego, does.

It is not a matter of mind over matter, or the reverse. Mind and matter are both necessary; they work together. The hand, the fingers execute the ego's plans. The adrenal gland produces adrenaline through which the excitement is felt that goes with the plan or the accomplishment; the gland is not the initiator of the deed.

The infinite and sublime outer products need interaction and mutuality, radiating and cooperating currents in all directions, combining all resources, to an end and aim conceived by the uniqueness of each individual—and the specialness of some. The talents in a brain are in its reverberating circuits. Cognitive and affective, ideas and feelings, the tight hemisphere and the left, cortices and basal ganglia fuse freely, supporting one another.

As Freud developed the science of psychoanalysis from the small to the global, from psychopathology to the normal, from symptom to character, from the individual to the group, from ego-alien to ego-syntonic, so do I suggest that our reflections on the process of producing a ditty might point the way to that which results in a symphony.

As from symptom to the dream, from a small thing might come at least the hint of some bigger conclusions. As I look back at these musings, I do not presume to resolve or even make a dent on the long-standing, Cartesian, dualistic, mind-body problem, which will take the most imaginative minds in history to solve. Certainly not from this small, personal, and relatively brief life experience (and experiment). But the mind, whatever this turns out to be in the long range with respect to concrete demonstrability and the further development of observing instrumentation, is an entity to deal with. The mind is indeed, following Descartes, the incorporeal substance operating under the laws of reason, and the body the corporeal substance operating under the laws of physics, but this does not, and need not separate the one person into dual entities. Both parts operate under the laws of reason, and both fall under the rule of cause and effect. Both are parts of the same total self. What we do know is that when the body goes, so does the mind.

CHAPTER SIX

Looking back

What happened?

What actually happened that day of my operation in 1995? The vascular complications conventionally feared by the medical profession, and articulated to every patient undergoing cardiac surgery, a major heart attack or stroke were gratefully absent at my surgery. But a less heralded complication came upon the scene. The vascular supply to the auditory apparatus was partially and temporarily compromised, sufficient to bring about a degree of malfunctioning in a susceptible system, already deficient and working below par, a neuronal tract which was the locus of least resistance to further vascular insult or insufficiency.

What we can postulate from the decade that followed, and the subjective experiences I have reported, is that it was mainly inhibitory circuits that remained permanently involved and reduced by the physical trauma, neuronal fibres that normally modulated loud external noises and kept them from impinging too strongly on the receptive, sensitive hearing apparatus. These, I suggest, were both those within the auditory pathways (contiguous fibres in every nerve are both stimulating and inhibitory; every nerve has both its stimulating effects and a built-in, limit-setting, inhibitory quality as well), and in the radiating webs of connections between the mid-brain and the temporal cortex, those that bring in conscious control. What was dominantly involved as a lasting residuum was the failure of normal inhibiting impulses that routinely reduced excessive sound for the comfort and protection of the individual. Every wearer of a hearing aid knows the emphasis by the distributors of these aids on the curtailing of ambient sound. A good aid can turn down the roar of a passing truck or mute the airplane engine in which one is a passenger.

A new problem added to my long-standing hearing diminution was an increased impairment of automatic inner limit setting. My hearing aids still provide external protection but what are lost are the upper limits on internal sounds. And these are not under voluntary control. When I am clear, and not thinking, and my mind is open, in comes the tinnitus hiss, "the noise in the machine" (from metabolic processes, movement of the air around us, inner, outer, who knows?). If I have to do something about this, I can only do what is active, i.e., do something, think something; I have no access to inhibiting, stopping doing, and doing nothing. This leaves the field open. The tinnitus goes on to rhythm, and if it keeps going, any superimposition that can serve the pleasure principle will do. In comes music, a tune, a song (from dipping down to past, unconscious memory and affect). Converting the formless but jarring and discordant noise into lyrical listening which can be enjoyable, even to the swaying of the whole participating body, by the mind that had been intruded upon, is a creative act.

That the original stimulus is an organic one does not override this entire phenomenon as a complex symptom. Even though it is based on such an organic component, what it went on to become is still ego-alien, i.e., a foreign body intruder, and is as unwelcome in its essence as any other symptom. It remains an uninvited guest, however much it is mitigated and lived with for long periods of time. And however much I have had to accept it as now part of me, still once in a while, after these many years, in a low moment, I might say, only half meaning it, "Enough of this! How long can I stand it?" But I quickly answer, "Forever". Because this is no different from ringing in the ears. It is that, only more so. Lots of people, maybe all people, have that, and know what it is. You have to listen to it. And to stop it, you just have to not listen. This is like tinnitus stepped up a notch or two. The next step is to make something out of the sound, and that is music. That is more pleasant than tinnitus. But that is also why it is more persistent; its' enjoyable quality is beguiling. You get to want it. That makes it harder to get rid of it. Ringing in the ears is less desirable, therefore more easily turned away from.

The foreign tunes are at their worst, i.e., the most intrusive, when the music is unambivalently unwanted. This is so on trying to fall asleep, and on awakening, in that order. Curiously, but now understandably, this symptom does not occur when I doze off involuntarily, which is becoming more frequent. That is, if I am reading, or just musing, or watching television, and fall asleep out of boredom or being tired, it is never intervened by the involuntary songs. It is only when I want and prepare for a night's sleep, and try to sleep, that the symptom appears and interferes.

Composer, conductor, now audience too

At the end, I can no longer say for sure that I am not a composer. It might be more accurate to say that everyone is, in the same way as each individual, in constructing his own unique dreams, is creative, making up original stories and scenarios. While not everyone is a Shakespeare or a Mailer, each person's creations are his own, crafted into some unique unit almost every night, difficult for someone else to make out. Everyone does this a great deal, not just a little. In the same way, almost everyone composes. Again not as a Beethoven or a Mozart, but whether aware of it or not, since its roots are unconscious, each human being dreams his own dreams, and marches to his own tunes. Everyone composes his own ditties, and enjoys them in his own private way. He taps or hums or whistles them, each in his style.

My housekeeper, who has worked in our family for decades, and had known my son Richard almost his entire life, told me, at around the time of his birthday, that she dreamed of Richard often. "I first know that it is Richard by his whistle- he always whistled while he did things". This brought that trait to my mind. I remember connecting Richard's whistling to another characteristic of his. I would wonder—and ache—about what he felt about his frequent seizures. He used to say, when they were over, with a seemingly neutral, philosophical look, "That's the way it is". I used to connect that attitude, of which I was in awe, to his frequent whistling. I will never know how much this was my thought or his.

But while I am not alone in creating unconscious products— besides symptoms, these can be dreams, unconscious fantasies, thoughts or songs—not everyone is as captive an audience to his own whistling or tunes for all time or to the same degree. Driving home one evening from a concert at Disney Hall, a friend, who hears well and not too much, said she could not get the waves of Mahler's 9th Symphony, which we had just heard, out of her head. But not long later, she said, "It's gone", attesting to the fact that she had not joined the ranks of the normal abnormal.

I have been living at a normal border, between the brain and the mind, with a magnifying lens that on occasions exposes and enlarges its interaction. As I walk along the Pacific edge, with a regular rhythmic step, on a clear, crisp afternoon, my hum becomes a cadence, I am adding some kind of music, and I search for words to go with it. It is not a success, perhaps a dismal failure. But some nonsense words and syllables do catch on and become integrated into a rhythmic melody. The composite sound, rhythmic sequence, tune and nonsensical words become structured, remains steady, and begins to roll on its own, i.e., it continues after I stop the inner humming, and I begin to hear it as an outsider. I feel quite up, as though I might have been in some creative endeavour. For half a day, I am listening to music that I think I may have made up. Later that evening, I listen again. I hear something similar, but not quite the same. The nonsense words are gone from memory. But the tune as well, as I come to recognize it, is not exactly what it was earlier in the day. It has merged into the theme music from The Bridge on the River Kwai, which has long been on my inventory, and which comes up many times. As I sing along, I see not me on my walk, but Alec Guinness marching across the bridge, with his head held high.

Attempt at a theoretical conclusion

It is a dozen years now that I have been observing and trying to understand my psychic innards, centred on one specific aspect of an infinite maze, my experiences, thinking and feelings in the auditory realm. From this close, continuous and detailed study, I have a picture for myself about how the brain and mind operate together in that particular aspect of life, which, one must admit, is a considerable slice of psychological living. It may also be analogous to other related mysteries or at least ambiguous areas.

From the vantage point of that intense and concentrated observation and study, I would like to describe what I am left with, and to present a brief conclusion about the current status of this personal auditory condition, which I have no reason to believe will change much in the future. A routine day with regard to these auditory phenomena, that has become built-in to my everyday conscious psychological life, and which I believe will be the case from here on in, is the following.

Every morning upon awakening, or at moments during the day of a vacuum in thinking, I become aware of a foreign auditory stimulus that gains increasing attention. This may be mild and temporary or demanding, peremptory and continuous. I become conscious of an ongoing, pressing sound that is on a spectrum that I have constructed from experience as consisting of the following sequence: swooshing air, the rush of air assuming some regular rhythm, gibberish or nonsense words attached to the rhythm, the emergence of a song, composed or remembered, lyrics to the song-actual and/or partly made up, and with these an affect brought on by or accompanying that "music". Where music actually begins on this spectrum of sound-noise is a question, a point at which a grey area becomes a fine line. This semantic puzzle is reminiscent of a similar question that occupied my attention in earlier years about another continuum—where psychoanalytic psychotherapy becomes psychoanalysis.

My entrance into this auditory sequence during a psychic "break" can be at any point in the series. My conscious attention can be drawn to this auditory stimulus at any stage of this series of sounds, and either stay at that stage or progress further. By now, I have come to understand that this depends on the state of my attentiveness, thinking process or fantasy life. If my mind is at or close to the onset of the psychic vacuum I mentioned, and devoid of "cathecting" (attending to) a subject, it will be at the swooshing end of the spectrum; further along, as time passes, it moves toward song; it can pause and reverberate continuously at any point. When any degree of specific thinking starts, the direction toward hallucinosis is quietly displaced.

I can initiate the thinking or fantasies or day-dreaming periods at any time, and bring the music to an abrupt halt.

With regard to tinnitus, that other auditory intruder that people report, whenever I think of or listen for that, whether near the beginning or the opposite end of this hearing spectrum, or even during attentive thinking states when the songs are absent, this more commonly experienced "ringing in the ears" is also present. This background sound is audible whenever it is listened for, either alone or accompanying the hallucinatory songs or even as a background during the stage of an active thought process. This fine-line, hissing sound seems to be the baseline reaction of the auditory apparatus to the very process of living within moving air, or as a living organism with moving parts both externally and internally, on the surface and within the entire body—part of the human condition. Comparable to what physicists refer to as "the noise in the machine", the constantly moving molecules of air around us, the flow of fluids and the heart beats and the functioning of organs within the body, provide a constant and steady incoming purr which makes its way to the ear drum. The band of this motion that is within the 20 to 20,000 Hz which the human ear is capable of hearing is always there. In the unconscious, this is perceived as long as there is life. In the conscious system, it needs to be attended to, i.e., met with attention.

Most people, or at least most adults, either have or can call up and become aware of tinnitus under certain conditions; this piercingly relentless, continuous sound is the irreducible product of the meeting of the person with his environment. In the forest, the tree has to fall for sound to occur. In life the impingements are continuous. Whether a response to constant movement in the external environment, or initiated by age-related deterioration of the hair cells in the inner ear, or a side-effect of medication, a steady sensation of sound is transmitted from inner ear to brain to the senses. Perhaps here one can allow a combination of otologists, anthropologists and philosophers to unite in speculating that man, the most advanced technological product on earth, with this 24/7, infinitely thin, clear and steady line, can be attuned, beyond the adventitious noises on the sidewalk on which he stand and walks, to the sounds of the constantly moving physical world of his surround and the 24/7 purr of the living world within him.

Coming back to my sleeping and waking states, my own organic-psychological auditory constructions are superimposed upon this more universal physiological phenomenon. On the occasions in which awakening is not accompanied by some sound in my automatic series (yes, this too happens at times), this is a sign that I am already immersed in the problems of living, attending consciously or preconsciously to what awaits me that day. This process, an indicator and precursor of a readiness to take care of things, works to avoid or prevent or over-ride, or make unnecessary, the automatic sound and the preludes to song. The brain is already supplied with its necessary activity.

Whether I wake up with silence, or with sound or noise (agreeable or discordant), or trying to make music, humming, rocking quietly, even if barely, or searching for a song that fits, or with what is already a tune, or a song or a medley or even a whole orchestra on stage in my head (the latter can be not disturbing but exhilarating, manicy, portending "wow, what a day"), my subsequent day's activities turn these away as I get on with my things.

The whole sequence is not all or none, i.e., that I have it and others do not, but a complementary series; it can be "more-or-less" there. Some people are clear, some may hum and tap, I am programmed more towards the tune-song phase than most. This might relate to the division of people I referred to previously; one group that awakes with "Good morning, God"; and the other "Good God, morning". The auditory experience of this decade moved me for a time a certain distance from the first to the second. But I can say that the first state has come back considerably.

As a final reflection, this un-sought experience has added several new findings to my previous studies in psychoanalytic theory, or the functioning of the brain and mind. The science of mental processes, steeped in the field of subjectivity, has generally failed to satisfy the criteria of the physical sciences to be evidence-based. This serendipitous long-range experience and experiment can now contribute empirical evidence in support of some psychological conclusions.

To this end, I would present the following formulations, supported by the evidential data described in this book:

1. The original disturbance was due to organic factors, affecting the auditory pathways of the brain, produced acutely during the

surgical procedure, which resulted subjectively in the experience of auditory symptoms of rushing (wind-like) noises. These were superimposed upon a previous chronic tinnitus, due to a more usual response of the auditory system to the sounds of living, from within and without.

2. The subsequent history of these unwelcome sensations came about by reactions and input of the mind, i.e., the agency of thinking, feeling and acting that derives from the brain but with the addition of accumulated life experience becomes the entity within the person that executes the wishes, intentions and decisions of the person into the external environment.

3. The mind worked on the unwelcome sounds, producing a sequence leading to music. At various times, it brought about intermediate pre-musical formations of rhythms, tunes and words that at their culmination became songs. These came from memory, choosing songs that fitted the affect and ideation of the moment, or by construction of new ones, from crude to better ones.

4. These songs, in line with psychological constructions in general, were seen to have meaning. Not the obvious meaning of each song, but a disguised, hidden meaning, as in a dream. The song, as any other artistic product, connects with a personal unconscious fantasy.

5. Such meanings—linked to the wishes in the fantasies—were unconscious, and came to consciousness with a feeling of surprised recognition.

6. The ability (the switch) to turn these songs off, as exists with consciously-produced songs or music at will, did not exist. They came from the unconscious, and control over them remained there.

7. They could be influenced to leave by conscious attention to other (consciously-initiated) music.

8. These combined findings confirm certain theoretical conclusions I have come to in previous writings from clinical end other observational data without such empirical evidence (Rangell, 1969, 1971, 1988, 1989).

9. This new evidence confirms a) that there is no completely free will. There is psychic determinism and partially free will. Will itself is both free and determined. b) that intention, purpose, "will", as recognized in conscious life, also exist in the

unconscious, outside of conscious control. This is the unconscious ego at work. c) that consciousness-the conscious ego-can acquire a degree of control over the unconscious process by learning, therapy and insight.
10. As the unconscious constructed the song, the same mechanism can apply to any creative product. The creative act, the filling of absent space by an image (by "imagination"), a function of the mind, depends mostly on this unconscious process. This applies to any modality, whether filling the unknown with words, a story, a poem, a novel—or with sounds, from songs to a symphony-or with forms and colours, a drawing, a painting, a building.
11. The utilization of this reservoir of unconscious creative energy is the challenge and opportunity of anyone who sets out to achieve in any field of creativity. As every artist knows, "Just let it come".

These conclusions present themselves to be considered from the observations and experiences of this decade of listening to spontaneous songs in my head.

The aftermath-where am I now?

Where am I today, as I reach my 94th birthday, 12 years after that physical handling (I will not say assault) of my vital body parts altered the smooth functioning of my most important organs, heart and brain? I have obviously benefited enormously, more than can be proven, from the direct results of the procedure. From the secondary effects, I feel that I know with a deep conviction a bit more about my inner control and its limits in a personal experimental situation, first passively then actively experienced. And I am here to tell this story.

I believe I have come quite some distance with a strange little disturbance that I first regarded with ominous curiosity as a potential major interferer with normal living. When I first encountered this intrusion, I conveniently, defensively, located it outside, coming from the hills, the sky, or some neighbouring building.

As I gradually came to recognize it as within me. I began to study it.

I first tried to eliminate the intruder, to cut it off. But I came to see its characteristics, that there was no turn-off button. For a short time, it alarmed me. I see in retrospect that avoidance of panic separates those many who succumb to the lack of control that comes with mental symptoms from those who labour at achieving that control. For some early nights, as I tossed and could not sleep, I wondered (I could use a stronger word) if I would go crazy, i.e., whether something from the outside would take over my mind. Without that, I was in for trouble.

I then watched carefully and began to apply my theoretical armament to this vexing and obviously lasting "thing". Ironically, I saw that any hope of understanding it resided in my very profession. And in my own previous theoretical preoccupations.

The by-then permanent study led me to other neuro-psycho subjects, which by contiguity I felt could be at least partially illuminated by these reflections. Trying to fathom the unconscious song led me to thoughts about the creative act. As I write this, a strange sense of *deja vu* comes over me, that I had not consciously thought of until now. That is that the subject of creativity is not a new one in my thoughts, but that in fact I have given it a central period of attention long before. I remember a paper I (1978) wrote and published on "The Creative Thrust" (a phrase I used above). I pull out the old paper; it pleases me in a big way. I wrote it in honour of a colleague, Dr. Harry Slochower, who early had been a college teacher of Anita's at Brooklyn College; his specialty was Thomas Mann. He later became a psychoanalyst, and a colleague, and re-met his student and now her husband. A meeting to honour him, held at the University of California at Santa Barbara in 1977 was the occasion for that paper, which was presented as the Opening Address to the symposium. My take on creativity in that work came via studying the roles of each structural system of the mind, the id, ego and superego, in producing the total, composite product—I gave many examples from art, music and literature.

As I read further, the paper was delivered on November 18, 1977. This was just a few weeks after the death of my son, who had died in mid-October of that year. How could I have gone? The paper surely had been committed to long before, and I (and Anita) went to the event. No wonder it was since then shrouded in forgetfulness. But it stayed with me, in the psychic realm-the unconscious- from which the music was now coming.

From previous writings, I also came back to my concept of "free will". For every adult person, this is a crucial area, how much of it is free, and the nature and quality of the rest that is given and determined. The combination of the two is what constitutes one's talent, his individuality, what one can expect of himself.

Gradually, my expanding orientation and increasing understanding of the mechanisms involved in the musical syndrome I was attending to led, in addition to a greater tolerance, to a more effective way to incorporate the new sensory stimuli without a grating interference with my ongoing mental life.

What I was experiencing became simply part of a vast array of normal phenomena, experienced by multitudes of people, humming, tapping out rhythms, tunes and songs. Freud (1913) compared the process of psychoanalysis to a game of chess. "Only the openings and end-games admit of an exhaustive systematic presentation . . . the infinite variety of moves which develop after the opening defy any such description". (p. 123). That is how it is with the kaleidoscope of automatic involuntary symptoms, and in more adaptive conditions, with the variety of paths open to creativity and will.

Today I harbour and own these tunes easily within me. I no longer regard them as unwelcome guests. They do not command much attention when they visit—no more than ringing in the ears in much of the population.

I in fact regard them as a good example of a generalization with which I ended my book (2004) "My Life in Theory": "Life is a combination of what has to be, and what we make of that." (p. 314). This last line, combining acceptance of our physical beings with full use of our mental facilities, has been made more indelible to me than even when I wrote it by a patient who told me that it has become his mantra in life.

Yet I am still always in for a surprise. This, in fact, is the name of the game, the purpose of the mystery, of the forgotten and ambiguous borders of every song, of the maintenance of repression. We do something to make up for, or make tolerable, something we do not want to face.

For a few days I am humming along a fairly spirited tune. When I stop to think about it, I rather neutrally conclude that I am just singing—the words then come—funiculi, funicula, funiculi, funiculaaaa—da, daratala, daratala daratala. It seems to define what I think is my mood—pretty good—things are ok—nothing to complain about—I believe it is fairly neutral—could be worse—hang in there … make the most of being alone tonight, free.

But I feel incomplete, compelled to fill in, there is more—the tune goes on, very lively—what are the words and phrases that precede the two that go on and on? I think it must be some popular American song.—I put the two known words into Google—what comes out? Luciano Pavarotti, live with the Chieftains—a crowd as far as the camera can see. As the orchestra booms, the greatest tenor of opera comes forward, starts to bellow out the famous and familiar Italian rendition, of which the only words I know are those two: funiculi, funiculaaahh—to the crashing climax. The crowd is screaming.

I am now worked up, emotional, strongly with the music. Why? Pavarotti died this week; his memorial was on TV over and over—but more—my brother, 2 years younger than me, died a few weeks before. A major emotional upheaval in my life and family. My brother often imitated opera.

This was a ditty that covered a sizzler. I went from neutral to being very upset. And I was glad about it.

I used to say the music was always present. I no longer do. I do wake up almost every morning with the beginning of a process; at least a swooshing noise, wind sounds, almost a challenge for me to decide which way it will go. Paying no attention is the best way for it to simply disappear. If you can just do that old Brooklyn thing: fergeddaboudit. I have learned to be able to do that. Listening to it starts some change, some advancing process. The sound becomes rhythmic; any further attention begins to play with the original more or less simple rhythm, which might start to become more complex and specific, preludes to something with a more definitive form. If I stay with it, some song might come along, make its claim, and begin to influence me, or start a mood, or at least make me aware of one. It might stay a while, or not, simply go away. Similarly, if I just think of or listen for tinnitus, perhaps just to test it, it is hissing at once, and can be quite forceful. I mostly can now laugh to myself, turn to other things, and my day at once gets to be free of this foolish distraction.

Similarly during the day: something is still there whenever I listen, and whenever there is a mental vacuum in which I am thinking of nothing. When a thinking task is just over, when I come out from a patient's hour, when I have a moment, perhaps on the way to a next encounter, to a group, to dinner, to talk to someone, either the rhythm, or the beginning of a song, or a more defined and insistent tune might come along, and seem to wish to stay there. It can become a tug-of-war between it and me. But such times are now by no means 24/7. They are only for minutes or seconds at a time, a number of times during the 24-hour cycle. And not with the same urgency or duration. And they do not bother me. The anxiety about their future is no more. I can almost always just go about my things—and poof: the whole thing is gone. I have some, enough control. And I can even enjoy them for a time, quite easily. I sing along. I join them. They are no problem.

Would that other mental symptoms can be helped the same way. Maybe they can.

REFERENCES

Arlow, J.A. (1969). Unconscious fantasy and disturbances of conscious experience. *Psychoanal. Q., 38*: 1–27.

Benveniste, D. (2006). The melody haunts my reverie. *Fort da, 12*(2): 30–34.

Beres, D. (1960). The psychoanalytic psychology of imagination. *J. Amer. Psychoanal. Assn., 8*: 252–269.

Beres, D. (1968). The humanness of human beings: Psychoanalytic considerations. *Psychoanal. Q., 37*: 487–522.

Brenner, C. (2002). Reflections on psychoanalysis. *J. Clin. Psychoanal., 11*: 7–37.

Blumenthal, E. (2007). It's life, in miniature. *Los Angeles Times,* October 27.

Erikson, E. (1956). The problem of ego identity. *J. Amer. Psychoanal. Assn., 4*: 56–121.

Fisher, C. (1956). Dreams, images and perception. *J. Amer. Psychoanal. Assn., 4*: 5–48.

Freud, S. (1950a). Project for a scientific psychology, *S.E., 1*.

Freud, S. (1900a). The interpretation of dreams, *S.E., 4–5*, 1953.

Freud, S. (1913c). On beginning the treatment (further recommendations on the technique of psycho-analysis), *S.E., 12*: 121–145.

Freud, S. (1916–1917). Introductory lectures on psycho-analysis, *S.E., 16*: 243–483.

Freud, S. (1923b). The ego and the Id., *S.E.*, *23*: 3–68.

Freud, S. (1926d). Inhibitions, symptoms and anxiety, *S.E.*, *20*: 3–179.

Gerard, R.W. (1959). Neurophysiology. In *American Handbook of Psychiatry*, Vol. 7, (Ed.), S. Arieti. New York: Basic Books, 1959, pp. 1620–1638.

Green, A. (1975). The analyst, symbolization and absence in the analytic setting (on changes in analytic practice and analytic experience)—in memory of D.W. Winnicott. *Int. J. Psycho-Anal.*, *56*: 1–22.

Greenacre, P. (1963). "The Quest for the Father. A study of the Darwin-Butler Controversy, as a Contribution to the Understanding of the Creative Individual". New York: International University Press.

Hannett, F. (1964). The haunting lyric—The personal and social significance of american popular songs. *Psychoanal. Q.*, *33*: 226–269.

Hartmann, H. (1939). Ego psychology and the problem of adaptation. Trans. by David Rapaport. New York: Int. Univ. Press, 1958.

Hartmann, H. (1950). Comments on the psychoanalytic theory of the ego. In *Essays in Ego Psychology: Selected Papers on Psychoanalytic Theory*. New York. International. University Press. 1964, pp. 113–141.

Hartmann, H. (1959). Psychoanalysis as a scientific theory. In *Essays in Ego Psychology: Selected Papers on Psychoanalytic Theory*. New York. International University Press. 1964, pp. 318–350.

Kandel, E.R. (2001). Genes, synapses and long-term memory. Address to the American Psychiatric Association, "Mind Meets Brain", New Orleans, LA, May.

Kety, S.S. (1960). A biologist examines the mind and behavior. *Science*, *132*: 1861.

Noy, P. (1996). Kissin the musical genius, *The New Yorker*, Aug. 26 and Sept. 2, p. 119. In *The Development of Musical Ability. Psychoanal. Study Child*, 1968, *3*: 332–347.

Rangell, L. (1952). The analysis of a doll phobia. *Int. J. Psychoanal.*, *33*: 43–53.

Rangell, L. (1967). Psychoanalysis, affects, and the "human Core"—on the relationship of psychoanalysis to the behavioral sciences. *Psychoanal. Q.*, *36*: 172–202.

Rangell, L. (1969). The intrapsychic process and its analysis: A recent line of thought and its current implications. *Int. J. Psychoanal.*, *50*: 65–77.

Rangell, L. (1971). The decision-making process. A contribution from psychoanalysis. *Psychoanal. Study Child*, *26*: 425–452.

Rangell, L. (1975). Psychoanalysis and the process of change: *Int. J. Psycho-Anal.*, *56*: 87–98.

Rangell, L. (1978). The creative thrust. A psychoanalytic theory. *American Imago*, *35*: 27–44.

Rangell, L. (1986). The executive functions of the ego. An extension of the concept of ego autonomy. *Psychoanal. Study Child 41*: 1–37.

Rangell, L. (1989). Action theory within the structural view. In *Int. J. Psychoanal.*, *70*: 189–203.

Rangell, L. (1990). *The Human Core. The Intrapsychic Base of Behavior.* Volume I: *Action Within the Structural View.* Volume II: *From Anxiety to Integrity.* Madison, CT: Int. Univ. Press.

Rangell, L. (1991). Castration. *J. Amer. Psychoanal. Assn.*, *39*: 3–23.

Rangell, L. (2000). Psyche and soma: Leaps and continuities. *Journal Clinical Psychoanalysis*, *9*: 173–200.

Rangell, L. (2002). Discussion of Brenner's "Reflections on psychoanalysis"— and parallel reflections. *J. Clin. Psychoanal.*, *11*: 96–114

Rangell, L. (2004). *My Life in Theory.* New York: Other Press.

Rapaport, D. (1951). The autonomy of the ego. *Bull. Menninger Clin.*, *15*: 113–123.

Rapaport, D. (1958). The theory of ego autonomy: A generalization. *Bull. Menninger Clin.*, *22*: 13–35.

Reik, T. (1948). *Listening with the Third Ear.* New York: Farrar, Straus.

Reik, T. (1953). *The Haunting Melody.* New York: Farrar, Straus and Young, 1953.

Sacks, O. (2006). The power of music. *Brain, 29*: 2528–2532.

Sacks, O. (2007). *Musicophilia. Tales of Music and the Brain*, New York, Toronto: Knopf.

Smith, L. (2007). Finding his ideas in dreams. *Los Angeles Times*, October 17.

Zilboorg, G. (1941). *A History of Medical Psychology.* New York: Norton.